ARCHAEOLINGUA

Edited by
ERZSÉBET JEREM and WOLFGANG MEID

Series Minor
40

GERGELY CSIKY

THE TRANSFORMATION OF PONTIC TRADE FROM LATE ANTIQUITY TO THE MIDDLE AGES

Transport vessels from the Archaeological Museum of Sinop

Institute of Archaeology, RCH
of the Hungarian Academy of Sciences

Archaeolingua Foundation

BUDAPEST 2017

The publication of this book was generously supported by
OTKA/NKFI grant no. PD 100177, "The Black Sea Trade in the
Early Middle Ages – Investigation of a Byzantine Harbour – Sinope/Sinop".

Front Cover

Aerial view of Sinop with amphorae in the foreground.
Photographs by Gergely Csiky (Sinop) and Ádám Bíró (amphorae),
photo editing: Zsolt Réti

Back Cover

The city walls of Sinope

ISBN 978-963-9911-96-3

HU-ISSN 1216-6847

2017

ARCHAEOLINGUA ALAPÍTVÁNY
H-1067 Budapest, Teréz krt. 13.

Desktop editing and layout by Rita Kovács

Printed in Hungary by Prime Rate Kft.

Contents

Acknowledgements

This volume is the outcome of museum research in Sinop. I first came into contact with Sinop through my Turkish friend, Halil Evren Sünnetçioğlu, whom I can never thank enough for introducing me to this wonderful town. Owen P. Doonan and Alexander Bauer welcomed me to their highly interesting project, the "Sinop Regional Archaeological Project" (SRAP), whereby I became familiar with the landscape around Sinop during our field surveys, which acted as a major source of inspiration for further research.

While working in Sinop, the museum staff was most generous with help in all questions regarding the region's history and archaeology. With his expertise, deep knowledge and understanding of the archaeological heritage around Sinop, Fuat Dereli was an inexhaustible source of information. Hüseyin Vural, Director of the Sinop Archaeological Museum, was very supportive and helped in solving all kinds of problems, ranging from museum research to organising our accommodation. Erdal Acar and Mehmet Çöndür, the museum's archaeologists, supervised our work in the building's basement in a very kind and agreeable way.

The museum research and my research trips to Sinop were generously funded by a grant from the Hungarian Scientific Research Fund (OTKA PD 100177; National Research, Development and Innovation Fund/NKFIH from 2014), without which an international project of this type would have been inconceivable. Ádám Bíró and Dávid Schwarcz, my colleagues in this project, were invaluable during the museum research in the Sinop Museum. Ádám took professional photographs of the artefacts from every possible angle, while Dávid helped with the description and evaluation of the metal artefacts. The three of us had a wonderful time in Sinop and working with them was not only a useful, but also a most pleasant experience.

Our research did not end in the Sinop museum. After completing the report and publishing preliminary studies as well as offering presentations at various conferences, the classification and assessment proper of the material was undertaken at the Institute of Archaeology of the Research Centre for Humanities of the Hungarian Academy of Sciences, which provided a wonderful research environment. I am greatly indebted to Professor Csanád Bálint for encouraging me to study Byzantine archaeology and to Professor Elek Benkő, our Director, for his constant support in the publication of this volume. During my work on the present book, I received technical support both from staff of our Institute and from the staff of Archaeolingua Publishers. All the plates in this volume were compiled and edited by Zsolt Réti, our institute's graphic artist. The text was translated into English by Magdaléna Seleanu. Rita Kovács of the Archaeolingua Publisher undertook the desktop editing of the manuscript. I am deeply grateful to Erzsébet Jerem of Archaeolingua Publisher for accepting the manuscript for publication in their series and for guiding it through the editing process.

Introduction

Sinope was one of the major harbours of the southern Black Sea coast during antiquity and the Middle Ages. Harbours are nodes in the network of maritime interactions, principally of seaborne trade. Maritime commerce offered a large variety of goods, from the supply of food staples to early metropolises such as Rome and Constantinople[1] to exotic, often luxurious commodities. As a result, harbours can be regarded as gates opening onto the outside world, as meeting points of peoples of various social, ethnic, religious and regional backgrounds, and as huge warehouses offering a wide range of commodities for the population. Thus, the significance of harbour cities should hardly be underestimated, especially in view of the fact that most of the antique and medieval metropolises of the Mediterranean (Rome,[2] Constantinople,[3] Antioch[4] and Alexandria[5]) had large harbours in their urban area or nearby.

It is thus quite understandable why the research of harbours became an immensely popular topic among both historians and archaeologists. This growing interest in ports and harbours is well illustrated by a DFG Special Research Programme in Germany made up of fifteen separate research projects on harbours from the Roman period to the Middle Ages,[6] among others on the Byzantine harbours of the Balkanic coast[7] and Byzantine harbour administration.[8] One impressive result of this research programme is a comprehensive catalogue listing over four thousand ancient harbours and ports,[9] and a Web-GIS system

---

1 These cities were fed with grain from Egypt via Alexandria as part of the *annona* system. For Constantinople, see Segré 1942–43, 393–444; Mango 1985, 23–50; Mundell Mango 2000, 190–193.

2 For Ostia, the harbour of Rome, see http://www.ostia-antica.org/, with the relevant bibliography (last accessed March 23, 2016).

3 For the harbours of Constantinople, see Magdalino 2000.

4 The harbour of Antioch is 20 km downstream at the estuary of the River Orontes; the site is called al-Mina, cf. Lane 1938, 19–78; Walmsley 2000, 295.

5 de Graauw 2000.

6 http://www.spp-haefen.de/en/home/ (last accessed March 25, 2016).

7 http://www.spp-haefen.de/en/projects/byzantine-harbours-on-the-balkan-coasts/ (last accessed March 25, 2016).

8 http://www.spp-haefen.de/en/projects/hafenverwaltung-im-byzantinischen-reich/ (last accessed March 25, 2016).

9 de Graauw 2000.

incorporating the geographical data on the studied harbours.[10] Additionally, various international workshops and conferences were devoted to this topic, whose papers were published in several volumes.[11]

One of the reasons for the upsurge of interest in ancient harbours was the discovery of the Portus Theodosiacus, the largest port of Constantinople, during the rescue excavations preceding the Marmaray metro construction begun in 2004 at Yenikapı in Istanbul. The excavations at Yenikapı brought to light thirty-seven shipwrecks dating from the fifth to the eleventh centuries, complete with their cargo consisting of various amphorae. The processing and assessment of this immense volume of finds is still in progress,[12] but its sheer quantity promises a major breakthrough in the study of late antique and early medieval seaborne trade.

While neither the importance, nor the size of Sinope's harbour can be compared to Constantinople's huge ports, it was definitely a prominent one on a regional Pontic scale up to the Crimean War (1853–1856). Sinope's prominence[13] can be sought in its geographic location[14] and diversity. The Sinop promontory (*Sinop Yarımadası*) is the northernmost point of Anatolia as well as the currently northernmost province of Turkey (officially called *Sinop İli*). The city lies at the intersection of the Black Sea's two major currents facilitating transmarine communication with the northern coast, especially with the Crimea.[15] The city's centre was built on the neck of the mainland leading to the volcanic cone of the Boztepe, while the greater part of the promontory is made up of sedimentary rocks (limestone and flysch).[16] The promontory's western and eastern shore differ

---

10 http://haefen.i3mainz.hs-mainz.de/spp/composer/ (last accessed March 25, 2016).

11 Istanbul 2011: LADSTÄTTER – PIRSON – SCHMIDTS 2015; Mainz 2013: PREISER-KAPELLER – DAIM 2015.

12 The preliminary results have been presented in exhibition catalogues: ÖZTUNCAY–KARAMANI PEKIN 2007; KIZILTAN – ÇELIK 2013. Monographs on shipwrecks: KOCABAŞ 2012; AKKEMIK 2015.

13 The city of Sinop in Turkey was called *Σινώπη* in Greek and *Sinope* in Latin during antiquity, therefore the form *Sinope* will be used for designating the ancient and medieval city up to 1214, the date of the Seljuk occupation, while the form *Sinop* for the modern Turkish city.

14 For the geography of Sinop, see TARKAN 1941.

15 For the effect of the sea currents on the settlements in the Sinop area, see ÖZDEMIR 2002, 74–125.

16 For the geography of the Sinop peninsula, see GEDIK – ERCAN – KORKMAZ 1982–83, 34–50; GEDIK – KORKMAZ 1984, 53–79; DOONAN 2004, 13.

considerably: sailing is difficult on the western side owing to the steep, rugged, rocky coast and the strong currents,[17] while the eastern shore provides an ideal agricultural hinterland[18] with its natural harbours and gentle hills.[19] The varied vegetation[20] and relief[21] form a colourful patchwork of eco-regions,[22] and led to the emergence of a wide range of economic strategies.[23]

Sinope became one of the main harbours of the southern Pontic shore from the Milesian colonisation in seventh century BC and retained its strategic role throughout the centuries of the Roman and Byzantine Empire. In spite of its prominent position in sea trade and naval warfare, Sinope did not grow into either a provincial or a *thema* capital. During late antiquity, the city was part of the province of Helenopontus with Amasea (Amasya) as its capital, while from the later seventh century onward, Sinope became the major naval base of the Armeniac *thema*.[24]

With its 27 ha large intramural area, Sinope can be ranked among the larger cities of the Pontus. The city's size also allows a rough estimate of its population,[25] which could hardly have exceeded five thousand.[26] This figure conforms to the pre-industrial population of Pontic cities; we know that Nesebar had a population of around four thousand in the nineteenth century,[27] and we can calculate the Ottoman-period population of Sinop from the tax censuses (*tahrir defteri*), which are available from 1487 and which in addition to the urban population, also

---

17 AKKAN 1975, 76; DOONAN 2004, 16.

18 DOONAN 2004, 21, 36, Figs 2–3, 39–40.

19 For the morphology of the eastern coast, see İNANDIK 1955, 21–45; İNANDIK 1957, 51–71; AKKAN 1975, 83–84.

20 For the region's vegetation, see DOONAN 2004, 18–19.

21 AKKAN 1975.

22 The typical eco-regions are Boztepe, the eastern coastal plain, the plain of the River Karasu, İnceburun and the western coast (DOONAN 2004, 36, Figs 2–3).

23 Fishing, cereal cultivation, horticulture (vegetables, fruits), olive cultivation, viticulture and transhumant stockbreeding (DOONAN 2004, 20–21).

24 BRYER – WINFIELD 1985, 12–13.

25 A coefficient of 200 people/hectare is generally employed (CHANDLER – FOX 1974, 5); more recently, Luuk de Ligt calculated with an average of 150 people/ha in his estimates for Roman-period populations, although in the case of Rome and Ostia, he used an extremely high coefficient of 300–600 people/ha (DE LIGT 2008, 147–154).

26 Using the median coefficient of 200 people/hectare, the estimated population figures are as follows: Amastris: 2084, Amaseia: 5346, Histria: 2696, Khersonesos Taurike: 6780, Trapezunt: 6088, Mesembria: 3156, Odessos: 9400 and Sinope: 5346.

27 VENEDIKOV 1969, 27.

contain information on the rural population, even if they only record the number of households. Calculating with five persons per household, Sinop's population was made up of 3735 Muslims and 815 Christians, adding up to a total population of 4568 in 1487.[28] The latter figure would imply that in this case, the coefficient of 200 persons/ha is probably too high.

Interestingly enough, the region's provincial centres did not lie on the coast. Sinope had administratively belonged to Amasea (Amasya),[29] even though their size was roughly identical. The agricultural hinterland of the cities was quite significant – the overwhelming majority of the population (80–90%) lived in villages during this period.[30] Obviously, the population figures specified in the above are rough estimates reflecting order of magnitude and should not be regarded as exact data.

Considering its modest size and population, Sinope did not boast a large harbour; however, due to the well-preserved city walls, the location of the city's harbour is exactly known[31] and its size can be easily calculated. It covered a 272 m long and 96 wide rectangular area of 26,112 m^2 (roughly 2.6 hectares), which is rather small compared to the excavated area of 58,000 m^2 in Yenikapı in Istanbul. The significance of Sinope's harbour is confirmed by the remains of a thirteenth-century arsenal from the Seljuk period, although the existence of shipyards is also reported in much earlier literary sources.[32] Beside the central harbour of Sinop, today known as Sinop Tersanesi, several other minor harbours, ports and landing places are known from the promontory (*Map 1*), including Stephane, Potamoi, Lepte Akra, Harmene, Karousa and Zagora, attested in both the *Peryplus Ponti Euxini* and the Ravenna Cosmography.[33]

---

28 Ünal 2008, 107, Tablo 13.

29 The city was first the capital of the province of Helenopontus and later the seat of the *thema* of Armeniakon: Bryer – Winfield 1985, 12–13.

30 For the low proportion of the urban population in antiquity, in contrast to estimates that it accounted for between 25 to 40% of the population, see Scheidel 2008, 31; for the Middle Ages, when, for example, the ratio of the urban population of England was 5 to 10 %, see Pounds 2005, 80. In the case of Sinop, the 1487 tax census records that 81.32 % of the population lived in villages (25,276 persons out of a population of 30,525 in the *kaza* of Sinop; cf. Ünal 2008, 107, Tablo 13).

31 Bryer–Winfield 1985, 88.

32 There is only a single reference to ship-building in Sinope, namely that according to the legend of Saint Phocas, the saint's father worked as a ship-builder: van de Vorst 1911, 260, 280; Belke 1996, 139.

33 For further details, see Csiky 2015, 328.

It is worth considering the nature of commodities transported to and from Sinope during the early Middle Ages. In the absence of written accounts, our main source of information remains the archaeological record that is mainly made up of shipwrecks, amphora kilns and the amphorae themselves. The commercial network of Sinopean carrot amphorae has been thoroughly covered by Dominique Kassab Tezgör, who demonstrated that Sinopean goods circulated not only in the Pontic, but also in the eastern Mediterranean, reaching even Syria and Egypt.[34]

What kinds of commodities were transported from Sinope in this extensive network? The agricultural products of the hinterland of Sinope have been discussed in detail elsewhere: suffice it here to mention olive oil production, viticulture and vegetable farming around Sinope, practiced from the Hellenistic period onward.[35] While Sinopean carrot amphorae were probably used for transporting wine and olive oil from this harbour, our knowledge regarding the late antique imports to Sinope and the continuity of sea trade during the early Middle Ages is much more limited.

The study of the early medieval period in Sinope is greatly constrained by a chronological problem. While the late antique pottery characterised by its black sand temper is relatively well known in the region,[36] the ceramic wares of the so-called Byzantine Dark Ages from the eighth–ninth centuries were completely unknown in the Sinope area. One potential solution to this problem is a comparison of the transport vessels stored in the Sinop Archaeological Museum (*Sinop Arkeoloji Müzesi*) with the amphorae and transport jugs from the northern Black Sea coast (Russia and Ukraine), where vessels of this type are often recovered from closed archaeological contexts and even the kilns of the workshops where eighth–ninth-century amphorae were produced have been discovered in the Crimea.[37]

Beside my overall interest in the region's geography and history, the main motivation for my research in Sinop was a personal one. In 2010, Halil Evren Sünnetçioğlu, one of my Turkish friends, asked me whether I would be interested in joining an American landscape archaeological project in Sinop. I immediately contacted Owen P. Doonan and Alexander Bauer, and thus became a member of the Sinop Regional Archaeological Project (SRAP). Both before and after the

---

[34] Kassab Tezgör 2010b.

[35] For further details, see Csiky 2015, 323–324.

[36] Doonan 2004, 15; Kassab Tezgör 2010a.

[37] Плетнева 1959, 241–244; Плетнева 1963, 50–53, Рис. 32; Якобсон 1979, 29–31; Паршина – Тесленко – Зеленко 2001, 53–79; Чхаидзе 2008, 145–152.

field walking with the SRAP in 2011, I spent several weeks travelling along the southern Black Sea shore from Karadeniz Ereğlisi (Herakleia) to Batumi, visiting all archaeological and regional museums (Karadeniz Ereğlisi, Amasra, Safranbolu, Kastamonu, Amasya, Samsun, Ordu, Giresun, Trabzon, Rize, Batumi).

After two seasons of field surveys with SRAP, I sought to continue an independent research on Sinope during the Byzantine period. I contacted Fuat Dereli, the former director of the Sinop Archaeological Museum, to gain an insight into the collection, and the new director, Hüseyin Vural, later also supported my plans. I successfully applied for a research permit for museum research in the Sinop Archaeological Museum from the General Directorate for Cultural Assets and Museums of the Ministry of Culture and Tourism of Turkish Republic.[38] The museum research lasted from July 3 to 26 in 2013, during which I studied 124 artefacts, including 61 amphorae, 26 jars, 19 metal artefacts and 18 pottery lamps dating from the fifth to the eleventh centuries.

Discussed in this volume are the artefacts directly connected to fifth–eleventh-century sea trade, namely the trade and transport vessels that could be assigned to this period.

[38] Permit no. 64298988.155.02 (YA.2013.06)–44/86.

The archaeology of trade in the Sinop area

The collection of the Sinop Archaeological Museum (*Sinop Arkeoloji Müzesi*) contains numerous finds that can be associated with trade, principally transport vessels, including amphorae. During the systematic study of the collection, I examined the amphorae dating from the late antique period to the eleventh century; however, I have deliberately neglected certain types. The so-called Sinopean carrot amphorae, the town's perhaps most distinctive ceramic product, were hallmarks of the wine and olive oil produced in the broader area. Dominique Kassab Tezgör's research identified the workshop producing carrot amphorae from the pottery kilns found at Demirciköy on the coast;[39] she discussed the typological development of the type and its distribution as well as its relation to other types in several studies and in a paper read at a conference on amphorae,[40] and later assessed all similar vessels in the Sinop museum, making a discussion of carrot amphorae in this study unnecessary.

Here, I shall only cover the imported amphorae (LR 1 and LR 2) of the late antique period from other regions found in the Sinop area. The transport vessels of the seventh to ninth centuries, of the so-called Byzantine Dark Ages, known from Sinop, which continue the traditions of the late antique LR1 and LR2 amphorae, have not been published previously, despite their fairly high number in the museum's collection. These shall be described in detail below.

The greater part of the amphorae dating from the Middle Byzantine period spanning the time from the late ninth to the thirteenth century have been treated in Nergis Günsenin's doctoral dissertation,[41] and thus in addition to the Günsenin 1 type (Ganos amphorae), I shall only discuss the tall-necked and flat-handled jugs (known also as the Tmutarakan type), which have been largely neglected in studies on the southern coast of the Black Sea.

Given these criteria and constraints, the discussion of the pottery wares of the late antique and early medieval trade of Sinop is essentially based on fifty amphorae and thirteen one-handled jugs. Sadly, the greater part of this pottery lacks an archaeological context; most were brought to the museum by fishermen working in Sinop and its broader area, who offered them for sale. In most cases, the findspot is simply specified as "Black Sea", although the entries in the acquisitions registers, the additional information provided by some fishermen and

[39] Kassab Tezgör 2010a.

[40] For a comprehensive discussion, see Kassab Tezgör 2010b.

[41] Günsenin 1990, 21–24.

the types of the amphorae presented at the same time does allow a few cautious conclusions regarding their origins.

Another consequence of the uncertain provenance of the amphorae is that their date can only be determined from a formal comparison with similar, already published pieces; one difficulty in this respect is that comparable pottery is little known from the Black Sea coast of Turkey or from Anatolia. In most cases, analogous pottery can be found in Russian publications of varying quality, highlighting the contacts between the northern and southern coast of the Black Sea.

The period between late antiquity and the High Middle Ages is generally described as an age of transformation, and this is also true of trade. The study of the transport vessels of the Sinop museum also seeks an answer to issues with a bearing on the continuity or transformation of trade. The number and diversity of the imported amphorae in the museum's collection, and the geographic distribution of the known parallels shed light on the extent of the trade network as well as on the intensity of the trade. The form, dimensions and, in particular, the capacity of the amphorae provide important information on whether metrology had changed between the late antique period and the Middle Ages. The mineral inclusions in the amphorae's fabric can, in some cases, indicate the continued activity of a particular pottery workshop.

As the period's main transport vessels, amphorae often bear distinctive marks referring to their region of origin or contents, and thus in addition to their description, the other main focus of the study is an examination of what type of commodities reached Sinop and from where, the intensity of the contacts, and whether we can speak of the decline or diminution of trade contacts during the early Middle Ages in this region.

Late antique amphorae

LR 1 amphorae

General description

Late Roman (LR) 1 amphorae were one of the most widely used transport vessels in the late antique period (fifth to seventh centuries), circulating across extensive areas. Ten pieces are housed in the Sinop museum: four of these can be assigned to the LR 1A pale brown or pale yellow amphorae made from clay tempered with fine-grained sand. These vessels have a tall cylindrical neck, an oval, ovoid, ribbed body and angular handles. They can be assigned to the fifth century. Six pieces come from a later period (sixth–seventh centuries) and represent the LR 1B type, which was tempered with pyroxene (black sand), and has a shorter ribbed neck, a cylindrical body with prominent ribs and curved handles with deep grooves down the centre.

Research history

The type was first distinguished by John Riley during his assessment of the amphorae from Berenice[42] and Carthage;[43] since the type was widely distributed in the Mediterranean and the Black Sea region, it appears in virtually all amphora typologies of late antiquity. The LR1 type conforms to Antonova IX,[44] Rădulescu 10,[45] Scorpan VIII,[46] Kuzmanov XIV,[47] Keay LIII,[48] Peacock–Williams 44[49] and Papadopoulos 2[50] in earlier typologies. Dominique Piéri distinguished two sub-types within the LR 1 type, LRA 1A and LRA 1B,[51] a sub-division that was further modified by Andrei Opaiţ, who distinguished a further

42 Riley 1979.
43 Riley 1981.
44 Антонова et al. 1971, 86–87.
45 Rădulescu 1976, 108–110.
46 Scorpan 1976, 163, Pl. VIII B; Scorpan 1977, 277–278.
47 Кузманов 1985, 18–20, Табл. 8.
48 Keay 1984, 268–278.
49 Peacock – Williams 1986, 185–187.
50 Papadopoulos 1989, 82.
51 Piéri 1998, 98–99; Piéri 2005, 69–92.

six sub-types.[52] Piéri examined the type in the context of the fifth–seventh-century wine trade,[53] while in later studies, Opaiţ focused on the type's origins, arguing that it had evolved from what he defined as a proto-LR 1 sub-type whose production began in Cilicia in the later third century.[54] The type's distribution in the Black Sea region has most recently been discussed by Andrei Sazanov,[55] who did not mention any sites on the southern coast.

Fabric and temper

According to the amphora database maintained by the University of Southampton, the hard fabric of this type was tempered with hard sand and often has inclusions of limestone and serpentine, occasionally displaying also some dark grains of pyroxene. Its colour ranges from pinkish-cream (7.5 YR 8/2–4) to reddish-yellow (5 YR 7/6).[56] These traits could also be observed in the case of the amphorae in the Sinop museum, although the mineral composition and the grain size of the fabric enabled the separation of several groups. Only fine-grained mixed sand was identified in the fabric of two amphorae (Nos 1, 3), while black pyroxene grains were additionally found in the fabric of three other amphorae (Nos 2, 4–5). Five LR 1 amphorae in the Sinop museum exclusively contained pyroxene, generally fine-grained pyroxene (Nos 6–9), and large, coarse-grained pyroxene in one case (No. 10).

Most of the LR 1 amphorae (six pieces) had a pale brown (Nos 1, 9–10), pale yellow (Nos 5–6), or light brown fabric (No. 2), although pieces fired to a dark grey (No. 7) or greyish-red (No. 3), and a brighter orange colour (No. 4) are also encountered. The colour of these amphorae ranges from 5 YR 6/3 to 10 YR 8/4 on the Munsell scale.

Formal classification and metric data

The form of LR 1 amphorae changed during the fourth to seventh centuries:[57] Piéri distinguished two chronologically distinct types: a Late Roman 1A, which

---

52 Opaiţ 2004a, 8–11.

53 Piéri 2005.

54 Opaiţ 2010, 1015–1022.

55 Sazanov 1999, 265–279.

56 http://archaeologydataservice.ac.uk/archives/view/amphora_ahrb_2005/petrology.cfm?id=236 (last accessed March 2, 2016).

57 Piéri 2005, 71–77; Reynolds 2005, 565–567.

he dated to the close of the fourth and the fifth century, and the LR 1B, a type used during the sixth and seventh centuries.[58] LR 1A amphorae are characterised by a slightly thickened rim, a narrow mouth, a tall, slender neck, angular, oval-sectioned handles with a rib down their centre, an ovoid, evenly ribbed body, and a round base with a basal knob. In contrast, LR 1B amphorae have a wider and shorter neck, shorter, round-sectioned handles with grooves down the centre, a cylindrical body and a round base, from which the knob disappears.[59] The collection of the Sinop museum contains four LR 1A (Nos 1–4) and six LR 1B amphorae (Nos 5–10).

The dimensions of these two sub-types are roughly identical, and variations could only be noted in a few instances. The height of most LR 1A amphorae ranges between 45 and 51 cm, their greatest diameter between 24.5 and 29.3 cm. The rim is narrow with an external diameter of 7.5–8 cm, the neck is 8–9.5 cm tall with a diameter of 7–8 cm, the handles are often as tall as 15 cm. LR 1B amphorae have a height of 44.5–53 cm and a greatest diameter of 22–27.5 cm. The rim is wider, with an external diameter of 7.5–9.8 cm, the neck is 7.2–9 cm tall with a diameter of 7–10 cm. Handles have a height of 12–13 cm. The height of the two sub-variants is identical, while the greatest diameter of LR 1B is slightly smaller and the type has a wider rim and neck, but shorter handles than the amphorae of the LR 1A type.

Ornamentation

LR 1 amphorae have a ribbed body, the only difference between the sub-types being how narrowly or widely spaced the ribbing. The neck of the LR 1A variant lacks ribbing, while the body is covered with roughly 1 cm wide, evenly spaced ribs and the base has a 2–3 mm large cylindrical knob with a diameter of 1.2 cm. The ribbing is more narrowly spaced on the shoulder and in the region of the body-base transition of the cylindrical body, and more widely spaced in the middle section of the belly on LR 1B amphorae. There are no painted *dipinti* or incised graffiti on the LR 1 amphorae of the Sinop museum.

Distribution and origins

The type was distributed across the entire Mediterranean and even beyond: LR 1 amphorae have been reported from the Atlantic coast and Britain from between

[58] PIÉRI 1998, 98–99; PIÉRI 2007, 299.

[59] PIÉRI 1998, 98–99.

the late fifth and mid-sixth century.[60] This was the most common type along the Upper Moesian Danube section in Serbia[61] and on most Mediterranean sites such as Beirut, Carthage, Marseille and Tarragona.[62] The LR 1 type is attested in Scythia Minor (Dobrudja) from the early fifth century,[63] and became the most popular amphora in the Mediterranean and the Black Sea[64] as well as in the Iron Gates region[65] during the sixth century. The type is known from Constantinople, Alexandria, Beirut, Zeugma (Gaziantep), Carthage, Marseille, Rome, Tarragona and Galicia in the seventh century.[66]

Constantin Scorpan suggested an Istro-Pontic origin for this type;[67] however, more recent studies, and in particular the evidence from petrographic analyses and the excavation of amphora kiln sites, have shown that the origins of the type lie in the eastern Mediterranean. Pottery kilns attesting to the production of this amphora type have been discovered on the Cilician coast in southern Anatolia at Ayaş, Soles, Karataş, Tarsus and Yumurtalık,[68] and major workshops have been reported from Paphos and Zygi on Cyprus too.[69] It would appear that amphorae were principally produced in Cypriote workshops from the later sixth century onward, and neither can it be excluded that the Cilician potters had moved to Cyprus and continued their activity on the island.[70] Several other production centres are assumed to have been active, for example Seleuceia (Silifke) and Arsuz in Cilicia,[71] as well as Ephesus and Saqqara in Egypt.[72]

---

60 Tomber – Williams 1986, 47–48.

61 Bjelajac 1996, 72–76 (Type XXI).

62 Reynolds 1995, 70–83.

63 Opaiț 2004b, 294.

64 Halmyris (Scythia Minor province): Topoleanu 2000, 134–135; Opaiț 2004a, 8–10; Антонова et al. 1971, 86–87; Якобсон 1979, 13–14, Рис. 2. 6, Рис. 3. 8–9 (Type 9); Сазанов 1989, 44, Рис. 1/5.

65 Bjelajac 1996, 72–76.

66 Fernández Fernández 2012, Fig. 2.

67 Scorpan 1976, 163; Scorpan 1977, 278.

68 Empereur – Picon 1989, 236–243.

69 Demesticha 2000; Demesticha – Michaelides 2001; Demesticha 2003. For an overview of the workshops, see Reynolds 2005, 565.

70 Piéri 2007, 300.

71 Reynolds 2005, 566.

72 Piéri 2005, 80, with an exhaustive bibliography.

Chronology

Between the early fifth and the early seventh century, this amphora type was transported in bulk to the western Pontic ports and the troops of the Lower Danubian *limes*,[73] with the latest pieces recovered from later seventh-century contexts, for example at the Crypta Balbi in Rome, at Alexandria and in Ireland.[74] According to Piéri, LR 1A amphorae can be assigned to the fifth century, while the LR 1B sub-types to the sixth–seventh centuries.[75] This chronological framework enables the dating of the Sinop amphorae. The dating of the later LR 1B amphorae is confirmed also by the Yassı Ada shipwreck that sank in the 630s (van Alfen's Type VII).[76]

Function

The widespread distribution of LR 1 amphorae can undoubtedly be linked to the prominent position of Cyprus within the *Quaestura Exercitus* military administrative system created by the Emperor Justinian in 536, which incorporated Cyprus, Caria and the Aegean islands as well as Moesia Inferior (the Bulgarian Danube section) and Scythia Minor (Dobrudja).[77] This also supports the suggested *annona* function of LR 2 amphorae, namely that Cyprus was tasked with supplying the troops stationed along the Black Sea coast and the Danube with wine.[78] Thus, this type generally contained wine, although olive oil can also be assumed in some cases.

Catalogue

LR 1A amphorae

1. Amphora *(Plate 1)*
Inv. no. 4.2.89
Reg. no. 2918
Find context: from the Black Sea, donated by Ergün Özcan, resident of Ayancık

---

[73] Opriş 2003, 53–59.
[74] Arthur 1998, 164.
[75] Piéri 1998, 98–99.
[76] van Alfen 1996, 198.
[77] van Alfen 1996, 211.
[78] Piéri 2007, 301.

Pale brown (10 YR 7/4) amphora tempered with fine-grained sand; hard fabric, dull tone when tapped. Slightly everted, rounded rim; relatively tall, cylindrical neck with three slightly prominent ribs; oval body with rounded base and a prominent semi-spherical basal knob. The slightly angular, oval-sectioned handles, each with three grooves down the centre, spring from the middle part of the neck to the shoulder. The body is ribbed from the lower handle attachment downward, but left plain within a 5 cm radius around the basal knob. A dark brownish-black residue covers the exterior and interior mouth.
H. 51 cm, diam. 31.83 cm, rim diam. 8 cm (ext.), 5.7 cm (int.), rim Th. 1.1 cm, neck diam. 7.2–8.5 cm, neck H. 8.3 cm, left handle H. 15.5 cm (ext.), 10.8 cm (int.), left handle W. 3.2 cm, left handle Th. 2.3 cm, right handle H. 16 cm (ext.), 11.3 cm (int.), right handle W. 3.4 cm, right handle Th. 2.1 cm, rib W. 0.6–0.9 cm, knob diam. 1.2 cm, knob H. 0.2 cm

2. Amphora *(Plate 2)*
Inv. no. 14.7.03
Find context: from the Black Sea, found during a US underwater survey
Reddish-yellow (5 YR 6/6) amphora tempered with fine-grained sand; hard fabric, clear ringing tone when tapped. Slightly everted, rounded and thickened rim; tall, cylindrical neck with three barely prominent ribs, wheel turn marks are clearly visible on the neck interior; oval, rounded body without any transitions, the greatest diameter in the vessel's upper third; rounded base with small semi-spherical knob. The angular, round-sectioned handles, each with a pair of deep grooves down the centre, spring from the upper third of the neck to the shoulder. The greater part of the body from the lower handle attachment downward is evenly covered with light ribbing, save for an area of 5 cm radius around the basal knob.
H. 49.8 cm, diam. 28.33 cm, rim diam. 7.9–8.1 cm (ext.), 5.3 cm (int.), rim Th. 1.35 cm, neck diam. 7.4–9 cm, neck H. 9.5 cm, left handle H. 15.6 cm (ext.), 9.8 cm (int.), left handle W. 3.2 cm, left handle Th. 2.4 cm, right handle H. 16 cm (ext.), 9.8 cm (int.), right handle W. 2.75 cm, right handle Th. 2.5 cm, rib W. 0.5–1.4 cm, knob diam. 1.3 cm, knob H. 0.2 cm

3. Amphora *(Plate 3)*
Inv. no. 7.1.1982
Reg. no. 2402
Find context: from the Black Sea, purchase from fisherman Recep Batman, resident of Sinop (December 13, 1982)
Pale brown (10 YR 6/3) amphora tempered with fine-grained mixed sand; hard fabric, clear ringing tone when tapped. Slightly everted, rounded, thickened rim; relatively short, plain, cylindrical neck; oval, ovoid body without any transition and a small hemispherical basal knob in the centre of the rounded base. The two angular, oval-sectioned handles, each with a pair of grooves down the centre, spring from the middle of the neck to the

shoulder. The body is ribbed from the lower handle attachment to the base, more narrowly spaced on top and at the bottom than in the middle.
H. 53 cm, diam. 29.28 cm, rim diam. 7.5 cm (ext.), 5 cm (int.), rim Th. 1.1 cm, neck diam. 6.8–8.5 cm, neck H. 8 cm, left handle H. 15.3 cm (ext.), 9.3 cm (int.), left handle W. 2.8 cm, left handle Th. 2.9 cm, right handle H. 15.6 cm (ext.), 10.4 cm (int.), right handle W. 3 cm, right handle Th. 2.8 cm, rib W. 0.7 cm, 1.2 cm, 0.7 cm, knob diam. 1.6 cm, knob H. 0.3 cm

4. Amphora *(Plate 4)*
Inv. no. 10.1.99
Reg. no. 3273
Find context: from the Black Sea, purchase from Mustafa Kaymak, resident of Sinop (Camikebir mah. Alan sok. 7) (June 7, 1999)
Reddish-yellow (7.5 YR 6/6) amphora tempered with fine-grained mixed sand and some fine-grained pyroxene; hard fabric, clear ringing tone when tapped. Short, slightly everted, rounded rim; relatively tall, cylindrical, plain neck; oval, ovoid body without any transitions; rounded base with a barely prominent round knob. The two curved, oval-sectioned handles, each with a pair of deep grooves down the centre, spring from the upper third of the neck to the shoulder. The body is ribbed from the lower handle attachment downward; the ribbing is evenly spaced and extends to the vessel base. The rim is coated with a shiny black residue, probably resin.
H. 45.4 cm, diam. 24.5 cm, rim diam. 7.6 cm (ext.), 5.7 cm (int.), rim Th. 1 cm, neck diam. 6.4–7.6 cm, neck H. 8 cm, left handle H. 11.4 cm (ext.), 6.8 cm (int.), left handle W. 2.9 cm, left handle Th. 2.6 cm, right handle H. 11.5 cm (ext.), 6.5 cm (int.), right handle W. 3 cm, right handle Th. 2.4 cm, rib W. 1 cm, knob diam. 1 cm

LR 1B amphorae

5. Amphora *(Plate 5)*
Inv. no. 5.1.98
Reg. no. 3213
Find context: from the Black Sea, purchase from Alsen Gerginci, resident of Sinop (July 16, 1998)
Light grey (10 YR 7/2) amphora tempered with fine-grained sand and fine-grained pyroxene; hard fabric, clear ringing tone when tapped. Gently everted rim; short, cylindrical neck with a wide, flat rib; cylindrical, barrel-shaped body with rounded base and a barely prominent, round basal knob. The two angular, oval-sectioned handles spring from under the rim to the shoulder. The body is ribbed from the lower handle attachment downward, but left plain within a 6.7 radius around the knob. The ribbing is

more narrowly spaced at the top and at the base, and more widely spaced around the belly. A regular hole with a diameter of 2.1 cm pierces the belly.
H. 51 cm, diam. 25.46 cm, rim diam. 8.7 cm (ext.), 5.6 cm (int.), rim Th. 1.5 cm, neck diam. 7.6–9.2 cm, neck H. 7.2 cm, left handle H. 13.2 cm (ext.), 8.5 cm (int.), left handle W. 3.4 cm, left handle Th. 2.3 cm, right handle H. 12.4 cm (ext.), 7.6 cm (int.), right handle W. 3 cm, right handle Th. 2.2 cm, rib W. 0.6 cm (shoulder), 2.4 cm (belly), 0.6 cm (base), knob diam. 1 cm, knob H. 0.3 cm

6. Amphora *(Plate 6)*
Inv. no. 3.13.73
Find context: from the Black Sea at Yakakent, purchase from fisherman İlyas Gün
Light grey (7.5 YR 8/2), white-slipped, thin-walled amphora tempered with fine-grained pyroxene; hard fabric, clear ringing tone when tapped. Short, slightly everted, rounded rim; tall, cylindrical neck with two triangular-sectioned angular ribs; cylindrical, barrel-shaped body, rounded shoulder and base, with a round, flat basal knob. The angular, oval-sectioned handles, each with a pair of two deep grooves down the centre, spring from under the rim to the shoulder. The greater part of the body is ribbed from the lower handle attachment downward, more narrowly spaced around the shoulder, widely spaced around the belly and narrowly spaced again around the base, which is plain on the half around the basal knob. There is a sooty residue on the vessel body under one of the handles. A series of deep incisions was made on the shoulder and in part on the belly.
H. 53 cm, diam. 27.53 cm, rim diam. 9.8–9.5 cm (ext.), 7 cm (int.), rim Th. 1.3 cm, neck diam. 8.6–10.5 cm, neck H. 9 cm, left handle H. 13 cm (ext.), 8.6 cm (int.), left handle W. 3.1 cm, left handle Th. 2.3 cm, right handle H. 13.2 cm (ext.), 8.6 cm (ext.), right handle W. 2.9 cm, right handle Th. 2 cm, rib W. 0.5 cm (shoulder), 2.5 cm (belly), 0.5 cm (base), knob diam. 1.2 cm

7. Amphora *(Plate 7)*
Inv. no. 8.1.81
Find context: from the Black Sea, donated by Mustafa Kemal Koca (also known as Tarzan Kemal)
Light brownish-grey (10 YR 6/2) amphora tempered with fine-grained pyroxene; hard fabric, clear ringing tone when tapped. Short, slightly everted, rounded rim; slightly conical neck with a strongly rounded rib immediately underneath the rim; cylindrical, barrel-shaped body with no indication of a basal knob. The slightly curved, angular, oval-sectioned handles, each with a pair of grooves down the centre, spring from the rib under the rim to the shoulder. The greater part of the body is ribbed, from the shoulder downward to the body-base transition; the ribbing is more closely spaced on top and at the base, and more widely spaced in the middle. The rounded base protrudes slightly.
H. 50 cm, diam. 25.94 cm, rim diam. 7.5–8.1 cm (ext.), 6.1 cm (int.), rim Th. 0.8 cm, neck diam. 7.5–9.8 cm, neck H. 8.85 cm, distance of rib from rim 2 cm, left handle

H. 13.7 cm (ext.), 8.7 cm (ext.), left handle W. 3 cm, left handle Th. 2.6 cm, right handle H. 14.7 cm (ext.), 8.2 cm (int.), right handle W. 3.2 cm, right handle Th. 2.7 cm, rib W. 0.8 cm (shoulder), 1.3 cm (belly), 0.6 cm (base)

8. Amphora *(Plate 8)*
Inv. no. 14.1.84
Reg. no. 2772
Find context: donation (April 22, 1985)
Light reddish-brown (5 YR 6/4) amphora tempered with fine-grained pyroxene; hard fabric, clear ringing tone when tapped. Broken rim; tall, cylindrical neck with three triangular-sectioned ribs; barrel shaped body tapering slightly towards the base; round base with a small flat knob. The angular, oval-sectioned handles, each with a pair of grooves down the centre, spring from the upper part of the neck to the shoulder. The body is ribbed from the lower handle attachment downward, more narrowly spaced around the shoulder and above the base, and more widely spaced around the belly. The base is smooth, without ribbing,
H. 47 cm, diam. 21.32 cm, neck diam. 6–7.5 cm, neck H. 8 cm, left handle H. 13.8 cm (ext.), 9.7 cm (int.), left handle W. 2.6 cm, left handle Th. 2.7 cm, right handle H. 13.6 cm (ext.), 9.6 cm (int.), right handle W. 2.6 cm, right handle Th. 2.8 cm, rib W. 0.4 cm (shoulder), 1.7 cm (belly), 0.4 cm (base), knob diam. 1.4–1.6 cm

9. Amphora *(Plate 9)*
Inv. no. 8.3.03
Reg. no. 3416
Find context: from the Black Sea, donation from the Turkish Coast Guard (*Sahil Güvenliği*)
Pale brown (10 YR 8/4) amphora tempered with fine-grained pyroxene; clear ringing tone when tapped. Short, gently curved, everted, rounded rim; cylindrical neck with ribs; barrel-shaped body with cylindrical middle part and spherical upper and lower part, no indication of a basal knob. The curved, oval handles, each with a pair of very deep grooves down the centre, spring from the upper third of the neck. The body is ribbed, with deep and wide grooves in-between, from the lower handle attachment to the base.
H. 44.5 cm, diam. 21.96 cm, rim diam. 7.7 cm (ext.), 5.7 cm (int.), rim Th. 1 cm, neck diam. 6.5–7.9 cm, neck H. 8.5 cm, left handle H. 12 cm (ext.), 6.5 cm (int.), left handle W. 2.8 cm, left handle Th. 2.8 cm, right handle H. 11.7 cm (ext.), 6.1 cm (int.), right handle W. 2.9 cm, right handle Th. 2.8 cm, rib W. 1.3 cm (shoulder, belly, base), Th. 0.5 cm

10. Amphora *(Plate 10)*
Inv. no. 3.6.012
Find context: purchase from Şükrü Özdemir, resident of Ayancık (March 6, 2012)
Pink (5 YR 7/4) amphora tempered with coarse pyroxene; hard fabric, clear ringing tone when tapped. Curved, everted, rounded, short rim; cylindrical neck with four triangular-

sectioned ribs; barrel-shaped body with rounded base and a small, barely prominent basal knob. The curved, oval-sectioned handles, each with three deep, wide grooves down the centre, spring from under the rim and sweep away from the body before joining the shoulder. The body is ribbed with deep, wide grooves in-between; the width of the ribs is roughly identical; the ribbing extends to the base, ending at the basal knob.
H. 46 cm, diam. 22.12 cm, rim diam. 7.8–8.1 cm (ext.), 5.7 cm (int.), rim Th. 0.9 cm, neck diam. 6.8–8.4 cm, neck H. 7.7 cm, rib W. 1.2 cm, left handle H. 12.6 cm (ext.), 7.7 cm (int.), left handle W. 3 cm, left handle Th. 2.8 cm, right handle H. 12.5 cm (ext.), 7.4 cm (int.), right handle W. 2.9 cm, right handle Th. 2.8 cm, rib W. 1.4 cm, knob diam. 1.2 cm x 1.5 cm

LR 2 amphorae

General description

Although Late Roman (LR) 2 amphorae were widely distributed, popular transport vessels during the fifth to seventh centuries, there are no more than four pieces in the collection of the Sinop museum. The type is characterised by a wide cupped or splayed rim, a conical neck and a globular body whose upper part is decorated with horizontal or slightly wavy combing. The base is rounded with a short cylindrical knob in the centre.[79]

Research history

The type distinguished by Riley during the classification of the amphora finds from Berenice[80] and Carthage[81] was widely distributed in the Mediterranean and the Black Sea region. The LR 2 type corresponds to Variant 2 of the Scorpan VII type,[82] Böttger B,[83] and Antonova XI–XIII among the Chersonesus amphorae of the Crimea[84] in earlier typologies. It corresponds to Kuzmanov's Type XX among the late antique amphorae from Bulgaria,[85] which was assigned to the transitional

[79] Opaiț 2004a, 11.
[80] Riley 1979.
[81] Riley 1981.
[82] Scorpan 1976, 160, Pl. VII. 4, 8.
[83] Böttger 1982, 1, 70, Taf. 1; 31–136; Böttger 1991, 157, Taf. 1.
[84] Антонова et al. 1971, 88.
[85] Кузманов 1973, 19.

Type I A-16 variant in Kuzmanov's later, better-known study published in 1985.[86] Ljiljana Bjelajac assigned the Serbian pieces to his Type XX.[87] LR 2 amphorae have been reported from the Aegean and the Mediterranean; Henry S. Robinson assigned the exemplars found in the Athenian Agora to Type M 272;[88] David P. S. Peacock and David F. Williams labelled it Type 43,[89] John K. Papadopoulos described it as Type 1 in the corpus of amphorae from Torrone,[90] while Simon Keay classified it as Type LXV among the Catalan amphorae.[91]

Piéri distinguished three sub-types among LR 2 amphorae (LR 2A-C), of which LR 2A-B represent the late antique variants, while LR 2C can be dated to the early Middle Ages (eighth–ninth centuries),[92] and shall therefore be discussed in the next section. The Balkanic distribution of LR 2 amphorae and their role in military *annona* was discussed by Olga Karagiorgou.[93] Several studies have been devoted to the origins of this amphora type and the workshops in which it was produced in the Aegean.[94]

Fabric and temper

According to the amphora database maintained by the University of Southampton, LR 2 amphorae have a hard, fine-grained fabric and a colour ranging from light buff (10 YR 8/4) to light red (2.5 YR 6/6). The fabric is often scattered with white limestone fragments and a little mica.[95] The LR 2 amphorae in the Sinop museum were tempered with fine-grained sand and, in one case, with grog (No. 12), and limestone in another (No. 13). All LR 2 amphorae in the Sinop museum are very pale brown and yellow coloured, corresponding to 10 YR 7/3–6 on the Munsell colour scale.

---

86 Кузманов 1985, 10, 62, Табл. I.

87 Bjelajac 1996, 67–72.

88 Robinson 1959, Pl. 40, Pl. 29.

89 Peacock – Williams 1986, 182–184.

90 Papadopoulos 1989, 83.

91 Keay 1984, 352–357.

92 Piéri 1998, 100; Piéri 2005, 86–88.

93 Karagiorgou 2001, 129–166.

94 Chios: Tsaravopoulos 1986, Figs 36–37; Arthur 1989, 82, note 2; Arthur 1998, 168; Cnidus: Tuna et al. 1987, 49; Halicarnassus (Bodrum): Williams 1982, 102; Opaiț 2004a, 11; Opaiț 2004b, 296; Argos (Kounoupi): Zimmermann Munn 1985, 342.

95 http://archaeologydataservice.ac.uk/archives/view/amphora_ahrb_2005/petrology.cfm?id=239 (last accessed March 7, 2016).

Formal classification and metric data

Although the form of LR 2 amphorae changed substantially between the fifth and seventh centuries, their basic formal traits remained constant. The most distinctive feature is the cupped, splayed or everted and slightly thickened rim and the globular body. The short, curved handles are round-sectioned and lack grooving down the centre. The main difference between LR 2A and 2B as distinguished by Piéri is the height of the conical neck: the short neck of LR 2A amphorae virtually blends into the body, while the conical neck of LR 2B amphorae is quite tall. This formal change occurred in the mid-sixth century or later.[96] The collection of the Sinop museum has three LR 2A amphorae (Nos 11–13) and one LR 2B amphora (No. 14).

LR 2 amphorae are large vessels with a large capacity. Their height ranges between 55 and 62 cm, their greatest diameter between 44 and 49 cm. They have a wide rim with an exterior diameter of 11–13 cm and an interior one of 8–9.5 cm. The neck of the LR 2B variant can be as tall as 9 cm, while the neck of LR 2A amphorae is shorter (6–7 cm). The cylindrical knob on the base is wide, with a diameter of 2–3 cm, but it barely protrudes some 1 cm from the vessel surface.

Ornamentation

The shoulders of these amphorae are decorated with deep horizontal (Nos 11–13) or slightly wavy combing (No. 14),[97] the latter being more typical of the late pieces, current from the later sixth century.

Distribution and origins

LR 2 amphorae were ubiquitous on sites along the Danube and the Black Sea coast as well as in the Mediterranean. This amphora type occurs frequently in Roman Moesia Superior (along the Serbian Danube section) and accounts for about one-half of the period's ceramic finds from Singidunum (Belgrade) and Viminacium (Kostolac).[98] LR 2 amphorae are encountered in the late Roman-early Byzantine forts of the Iron Gates region (Saldum, Bosman, Ravna, Taliata/Donji Milanovac, Hajdučka Vodenica, Transdierna/Tekija, Diana/Karataš, Rtkovo, Milutinovac, Ušće Slatinske reke, Mihailovac and Aquae/Prahovo),[99] and it has

96 Piéri 1998, 100; Piéri 2005, 86–89.
97 For the variants, see Piéri 2005, 86–89.
98 Popović 1988, 13–15.
99 Bjelajac 1996, 69–72.

also been reported from the town of Iustiniana Prima (Caričin Grad) too.[100] The pottery from the late antique forts along the Lower Danube is dominated by this type, as indicated by the ceramic inventory from Sadovec-Golemanovo Kale,[101] Iatrus-Krivina,[102] Nicopolis ad Istrum,[103] Novae,[104] Pernik[105] and Dichin[106] in Bulgaria. LR 2 amphorae abound in the late antique province of Scythia Minor in the Danube Delta region (modern Dobrudja):[107] variants representing the same type have been brought to light during the excavations at Sacidava,[108] Tomis,[109] Histria,[110] Sucidava and Mangalia.[111] LR 2 amphorae are often encountered in the western basin of the Black Sea, thus on the Bulgarian coast (Bizone, Kaliakra and Varna),[112] in Moldavia,[113] in the Crimea and on the Taman Peninsula.[114] These amphorae are known in the eastern part of the Black Sea too[115] and on the western Turkish coast as far as Sinop.[116] Although the above would suggest a typical Pontic and Danubian distribution, the type has been reported from Constantinople,[117] the Aegean, both from the mainland and the islands (Athenian Agora,[118] Yassı Ada

[100] Bikić – Ivanišević 2012, Fig. 3.7, 42–44.

[101] Mackensen 1992, 239–242.

[102] Böttger 1974, 131–136.

[103] Falkner 1999, 252, Fig. 8.4 (Type 94 = LR 2).

[104] Кузманов 1985, 11, Табл. 1.

[105] Чангова et al. 1981, Fig. 61.

[106] Swan 2004, 371–382.

[107] For the type's distribution in Dobrudja, see Topoleanu 2000, 133–135; Opaiţ 1996; Opaiţ 2004a, 10–12; Opaiţ 2004b, 295–296; Opriş 2003, 59–64. The type was widely distributed from Britain to the Black Sea (Piéri 2005, 89, Fig. 47) and in Galicia in Spain (Fernández Fernández 2012, Fig. 2).

[108] Scorpan 1977, 275, Fig. 10. 4.

[109] Scorpan 1977, 275, Fig. 10. 8.

[110] Condurachi et al. 1954, 459, Fig. 383.

[111] Scorpan 1976, 160, note 23.

[112] Кузманов 1985, 11.

[113] Рикман et al. 1971, 101–102, Рис. 20.

[114] Антонова et al. 1971, 88; Якобсон 1970, 30, 32, Рис. 2. 1–3, 6, 7; Якобсон 1979, 14, 10, Рис. 2, 7, Рис. 3. 2–3; Сазанов 1989, 46.

[115] Pitiunt: Рамишвили 1965, 114, Рис 6; Гамбашидзе 1963, Табл. I. 3; Бердзенишвили – Путуридзе 1975, Рис. 58, Табл. 62. 4.

[116] Csiky 2012, 5.

[117] Saraçhane: Hayes 1992, 62–71, Fig. 22. 8, 10–11.

[118] Robinson 1959, 109, Pl. 29.

Shipwreck 2,[119] Chios,[120] Samos,[121] Thasos[122] and Torone[123]), as well as from other regions in the Mediterranean.[124] The type's presence in the amphora corpus from Carthage increases visibly in the later sixth century, although its use appears to have declined by the mid-seventh century.[125]

Scorpan believed that these amphorae originated from the Istro-Pontic region, i.e. from the Danube and the Black Sea region;[126] however, as Tivadar Vida correctly pointed out, the type could equally well have originated from the Aegean or the Mediterranean.[127] Pottery kilns for firing LR 2 amphorae have recently been excavated on Chios[128] and at Cnidus,[129] indicating the presence of workshops producing these amphorae. However, other evidence, principally from petrographic studies, suggests that amphorae of this type were also manufactured in Bodrum (Halicarnassus) in Anatolia[130] and in the Kounoupi area in Argos, where amphora kilns have been uncovered.[131] In the lack of petrographic studies, it is impossible to determine in which of the above workshops the Sinop amphorae had been produced – what seems quite certain is that they originated from the Aegean.

Chronology

Although LR 2A amphorae had already appeared at the close of the fourth century, they became truly widespread in the fifth century. Their use continued

---

[119] BASS – van DOORNINCK 1982, 157.

[120] BALLANCE et al. 1989, 106f, Nos 236–239, Pl. 24–25.

[121] HAUTUMM 1981, Abb. 24–25.

[122] ABADIE-REYNAL – SODINI 1992, 56–57.

[123] PAPADOPOULOS 1989, 83–102. For the Aegean distribution, see KARAGIORGOU 2001, 139–145.

[124] For the western Mediterranean distribution, see KEAY 1984, 352–357; for the distribution of LR 2 amphorae, see SCORPAN 1976; SCORPAN 1977; RILEY 1979, 218, Abb. 44; PEACOCK 1984, 19, Abb. 4; BÖTTGER 1982, 39, 91 Karte 1; KEAY 1984, 661; PEACOCK – WILLIAMS 1986, 182f, Fig. 102; MACKENSEN 1987, 249. For an illustration of their distribution, see PIÉRI 2005, 89, Fig. 47.

[125] RILEY 1981; PEACOCK 1984.

[126] SCORPAN 1976, 161–162, Pl. XXXII; SCORPAN 1977, 275–276, Fig. 11.

[127] VIDA 1999, 93.

[128] TSARAVOPOULOS 1986, Figs 36–37; ARTHUR 1989, 82, note 2; ARTHUR 1998, 168.

[129] TUNA et al. 1987, 49.

[130] WILLIAMS 1982, 102; OPAIȚ 2004a, 11; OPAIȚ 2004b, 296.

[131] ZIMMERMANN MUNN 1985, 342ff.

up to the mid-sixth century, when they were replaced by the LR 2B variant.[132] LR 2B amphorae were the main cargo of the Yassı Ada shipwreck, sunk near Halicarnassus in Caria, which could be dated to after 625/626 by a coin of Heraclius.[133]

Function

LR 2 amphorae generally have an extraordinarily high capacity of between 40 and 57 litres,[134] which was also noted in the case of the amphora found in the Avar burial uncovered at Kunbábony (which, according to Elvira H. Tóth's measurement, had a capacity of 53 litres).[135] These vessels were principally used for transporting olive oil, as suggested by the greasy touch of the inner side of some fragments assigned to this type[136] and the painted inscriptions (*tituli picti*) referring to olive oil occurring on some amphorae;[137] Karagiorgou argued that in addition to the foregoing, the vessel form, and especially the rim form, and the large capacity too supported this interpretation.[138] It is also possible that some amphorae were used for transporting wine.[139]

It is generally assumed that LR 2 amphorae were the transport vessels of the late Roman-early Byzantine military *annona* and that they were used for transporting olive oil to the troops stationed along the Danubian *limes*. In contrast, both Burkhardt Böttger[140] and Karagiorgou[141] argued that LR 1 amphorae with a smaller capacity were used for transporting wine, as suggested by their frequent occurrence on military settlements (principally forts).

---

132 Piéri 1998, 100; Piéri 2005, 86–89.
133 Bass – van Doorninck 1982, 157.
134 Opriş 2003, 60; Opaiţ 2004a, 11.
135 Tóth – Horváth 1992, 58.
136 Hautumm 1981, 47.
137 Opaiţ 2004a, 12; Opaiţ 2004b, 297.
138 Karagiorgou 2001, 146–149.
139 Based on the *dipinto* of an amphora from Tomis: Scorpan 1976, 162; Arthur 1998, 169; Piéri 2005, 93.
140 Böttger 1990, 926, cited by Curta 2004, 187.
141 Karagiorgou 2001, 149–156.

11. Amphora *(Plate 11)*
Inv. no. 3.2.012
Find context: from the Black Sea, purchase from Şükrü Özdemir, resident of Ayancık (March 6, 2012)
Yellowish-brown (10 YR 7/6) amphora tempered with fine-grained mixed sand; hard fabric, clear ringing tone when tapped. Large, wide, cupped rim with curved, rounded interior and an interior groove with thickened edge; conical, downward widening neck; wide, globular body. The short, bowed, plain, oval-sectioned handles spring from the middle part of the neck to the shoulder. A 17 cm wide zone of evenly spaced ribbing with slender, deep grooves in-between begins slightly above the lower handle attachment.
H. 55.5 cm, diam. 45.83 cm, rim diam. 11.9 cm (ext.), 8.1 cm (int.), rim H. 5.3 cm, rim Th. 1.7 cm, neck diam. 8–15.5 cm, left handle H. 12.8 cm (ext.), 6.9 cm (int.), left handle W. 3.3 cm, left handle Th. 2.4 cm, right handle H. 13 cm (ext.), 7.2 cm (int.), right handle W. 3.3 cm, right handle Th. 2.4 cm, rib W. 0.2–0.3 cm

12. Amphora *(Plate 12)*
Inv. no. 10.1.76
Find context: from the Black Sea, purchase from Dr. İbrahim Önder, resident of Sinop (Sakarya caddesi)
Dull yellowish-orange (10 YR 7/4) amphora tempered with grog and coarse-grained mixed sand; hard fabric (can be scratched with one's nail), clear ringing tone when tapped. Cupped thickened rim with a deep slender groove under the rim and a curved groove around the rim interior; short, squat, downward widening, conical neck; globular body with the greatest diameter in the upper third and rounded base with a prominent cylindrical, rounded knob in the centre. The oval-sectioned handles spring from the middle part of the neck to above the shoulder. The body is covered with narrowly spaced ribbing with slender, deep grooves in-between from the lower handle attachment to the greatest diameter. The width of the ribbed band is 13.6 cm.
H. 55 cm, diam. 43.9 cm, rim diam. 10.9 cm (ext.), 8.3 cm (int.), rim H. 5.6 cm, rim Th. 1.3 cm, neck diam. 8.1–14.5 cm, neck H. 6.7 cm, left handle H. 13 cm (ext.), 7.5 cm (int.), left handle W. 3.3 cm, left handle Th.2.2 cm, right handle H. 12.8 cm (ext.), 7.5 cm (int.), right handle W. 3.3 cm, right handle Th. 2.2 cm, rib W. 0.3 cm, knob diam. 2.6 cm, knob H. 1.3 cm

13. Amphora *(Plate 13)*
Inv. no. 36.6.77
Reg. no. 2091
Find context: from the Black Sea, purchase from Dr. İbrahim Önder, resident of Sinop (Sakarya caddesi, July 12, 1977)
Dull yellowish-orange (10 YR 7/3) amphora tempered with fine-grained mixed sand and lime; hard fabric, clear ringing tone when tapped. Tall, strongly everted, thickened, cupped rim; short downward widening conical neck; flattened globular body with the greatest diameter in the upper third; rounded base with a prominent semi-spherical knob in the centre. The bowed oval-sectioned handles spring from the middle of the neck to above the shoulder. The body is covered with an 18 cm wide band of ribbing with slender, deep grooves in-between from the lower handle attachment to the greatest diameter. The lower vessel half is smooth and unribbed. There is a wide circumferential groove under the ribbing.
H. 62 cm, diam. 48.2 cm, rim diam. 13 cm (ext.), 9.4 cm (int.), rim H. 6 cm, rim Th. 1.8 cm, neck diam. 9.3–16 cm, neck H. 7.2 cm, left handle H. 14.3 cm (ext.), 8.8 cm (int.), left handle W. 3.8 cm, left handle Th. 2.6 cm, right handle H. 14.6 cm (ext.), 8.4 cm (int.), right handle W. 4 cm, right handle Th. 2.8 cm, rib W. 0.2 cm, knob diam. 3.1 cm, knob H. 1.1 cm

14. Amphora *(Plate 14)*
Inv. no. 14.1.75
Reg. no. 1867
Find context: from the Black Sea, purchase from Nihat Kayas through the mediation of Nurettin Zarflıoğlu (September 25, 1975)
Dull yellowish-orange (10 YR 7/3) amphora tempered with fine-grained sand; hard fabric, clear ringing tone when tapped. High, thickened, rounded, cupped rim with a groove around the rim interior; relatively tall, downward widening conical neck; flattened globular body with the greatest diameter in the upper third; rounded base with a strongly prominent hemispherical knob in the centre. The bowed, oval-sectioned handles spring from the upper part of the neck to above the shoulder. The body is covered with slightly wavy, narrowly spaced ribbing with deep, slender grooves in-between. There is a wide, shallow groove underneath the ribbing.
H. 62 cm, diam. 45 cm, rim diam. 11.6 cm (ext.), 8.6 cm (int.), rim H. 5 cm, rim Th. 1.5 cm, neck diam. 8.4–14.5 cm, neck H. 8.8 cm, left handle H. 11.6 cm (ext.) 12.8 cm (int.), left handle W. 3.9 cm, left handle Th. 2.4 cm, right handle H. 13.5 cm (ext.), 8 cm (int.), right handle W. 4 cm, right handle Th. 2.6 cm, decorated band W. 21 cm, rib W. 0.2 cm, groove W. 2.2 cm, knob diam. 1.8 cm, knob H. 0.7 cm

Early medieval amphorae (seventh–ninth centuries)

The period between the seventh and ninth centuries of Byzantine history is often labelled the "Byzantine Dark Ages" owing to the scarcity of sources, both written and archaeological. This roughly two-hundred-year-long period was, until recently, a blank spot in the Anatolian archaeological record, not least because the occupation levels and layers post-dating the late antique period were most often simply destroyed during the excavations of major late antique cities. There is but one single excavation in Anatolia that specifically targets this period. Rich eighth–ninth-century layers have been uncovered in Amorium;[142] however, this area lies quite far from the coastal regions and thus the finds from this site are of little help in dating amphorae. Similarly, despite the major advances made in the identification of "Dark Age" pottery from Sagalassos, these have little relevance for amphora studies.[143]

Two types of early medieval amphorae of the seventh–ninth centuries can be found in the collection of the Sinop Archaeological Museum: both continue the distinctive LR 1 and LR 2 forms. Late variants of LR 1 amphorae differ from their late antique predecessors in terms of their temper and, in part, their form. In the eighth–ninth centuries, these vessels were produced in workshops located in the mountainous regions of the Crimea. The late variants of the globular LR 2 amphorae of the seventh and eight centuries differ from the fifth–sixth-century predecessors regarding their form. Proceeding in a chronological order, I shall first discuss the late globular amphorae (LR 2C) and then the late variants of the LR 1 form, the so-called Crimean amphorae (sometimes inaccurately termed Saltovo amphorae).

Late LR 2 amphorae (LR 2C)

General description

The collection of the Sinop museum has seven globular amphorae tempered with fine-grained sand fired to an orange or red colour. The amphorae have a short, strongly everted rim, a downward flaring conical neck, two small oval handles set on the shoulder and lightly combed bundles of lines on the upper third of

[142] Lightfoot – Lightfoot 2006.

[143] Vionis – Poblome – Waelkens 2009, 147–165.

the body. Although some of these traits can also be noted on late antique LR 2 amphorae, the differences between the two variants are substantial (a shorter rim, a longer neck, light decoration arranged in bands).

Research history

These amphorae represent a late variant of LR 2 amphorae and their study is thus closely intertwined with research on that type. The occurrence of globular amphorae with long conical neck in early medieval contexts was first noted on the Crimean Peninsula.[144] Anatolii Iakobson labelled these amphorae as Variant 3 of the Black Sea (*причерноморские*) amphorae, and described them as having a rounded ovoid form (*округло-яйцевидный*). He highlighted their tall neck, the decoration of the body arranged in bands and their large size. He quoted comparable vessels from the Kerch and Taman Peninsulas, as well as from the Don region (Sarkel and Karnaukhov) and the northern Donets valley, which he dated to the eighth–ninth centuries, noting that this type did not occur among the products of the Crimean amphora workshops (Chaban-Kule and Kanakskaia Balka).[145] The type was discussed by Svetlana Pletneva too in her assessment of the pottery from Sarkel, although she dated this type to the turn of the tenth and eleventh centuries.[146]

A high number of the late, long-necked variant of LR 2 amphorae was recovered from the seventh-century Yassı Ada shipwreck (719 pieces), which inspired studies on the form and metrology of these vessels that principally focused on the capacity and standardisation of these amphorae.[147] Piéri labelled this amphora type LR 2C and identified it with the globular (*globulaire*) amphorae produced in North Africa, Italy and the Levant. He dated the type to the eighth–ninth centuries.[148]

Looking at the Balkanic distribution of LR 2 amphorae, Karagiorgou interpreted the type as part of the military *annona*. She too distinguished a long-necked variant typical for the seventh century based on the amphora finds from the Yassı Ada shipwreck, the north-western fortification tower of Emporio on Chios and a seventh-century cistern on Samos. In her view, LR 2 amphorae underwent

---

[144] Якобсон 1951, 331, Рис. 4/20, 333.

[145] Якобсон 1979, 31, Рис. 13, 5–8, 32.

[146] Плетнева 1959, 243, Рис. 29/5, 244.

[147] Bass – Van Doorninck 1982; Van Alfen 1996; Van Alfen 2015.

[148] Piéri 1998, 100; Piéri 2005, 88–89.

the formal change in the later sixth century.[149] Karagiorgou later stressed the importance of distinguishing a LR 2a and a LR 2b variant within the main type.[150]

In her discussion of trade in the "Byzantine Dark Ages", Pamela Armstrong highlighted the fact that LR 1, LR 2 and red-slipped North African vessels generally occur together in the seventh-century pottery assemblages from the Aegean, citing Corinth, Thasos and Kea as examples.[151] However, she did acknowledge that in cases when there are no fine wares or coins for a more precise chronological attribution, a date in the eighth–ninth century can be plausibly suggested.[152]

Fabric and temper

All the amphorae assigned to the type were tempered with fine-grained mixed sand and fired to an orange or brick red colour (5 YR 6/6–10 YR 6/6). Unlike the typical late antique LR 2 amphorae, the fabric of these vessels contains neither mica nor limestone, and their colour has a darker and more reddish hue than the early variants.

Form and dimensions

The most distinctive formal traits of this amphora type are as follows: a short, rounded, slightly everted rim, a tall, conical neck, a wide, globular body and a round base, usually lacking a basal knob.

These amphorae are large vessels with a height of around 50 cm (49.5–57.5 cm) and a greatest diameter of around 39 cm (39.15–39.47 cm). The rim is narrow, with an exterior diameter of 7.5–8.5 cm and an interior diameter of 5.2–6.5 cm, meaning that they could be relatively easily sealed. The rim height is less than 1 cm and its thickness is around 1 cm, an indication of their small size. The neck is usually around 10 cm tall, with a diameter of 6.6–7.8 cm under the rim and a diameter of 10–12 cm at the base. The length of the oval-sectioned (3.5 x 2.5 cm) handles is around 15 cm.

The dimensions of the amphorae assigned to this category are highly similar, suggesting a standardisation of their capacity, a point made also by Van Alfen after his study of the Yassı Ada amphorae.[153]

---

[149] KARAGIORGOU 2001, 131–132.

[150] KARAGIORGOU 2009, 41–42.

[151] ARMSTRONG 2009, 176, note 83.

[152] ARMSTRONG 2009, 176.

[153] VAN ALFEN 1996.

Ornamentation

LR 2B amphorae are typically decorated with ribbing and deeply combed grooves in-between on the upper part of the globular body, which could be slightly wavy from the late sixth century. Good examples can be quoted from Svetinja (Viminacium),[154] Murighiol,[155] Kunszentmiklós-Bábonypuszta,[156] Chios and the seventh-century shipwreck of Yassı Ada,[157] all of which date from the close of the sixth or the seventh century.

However, this ornamentation does not appear on the Sinop amphorae assigned to this category, which are generally decorated in one of two ways: lightly combed bundles of lines on the shoulder or ribbing with wide, shallow grooves in-between. The two are occasionally combined and some amphorae also have graffiti incised after firing on their shoulder.

Combed decoration in bands can be noted on three amphorae (Nos 16–18), while on one piece (No. 21), the combing is deeper and more pronounced than on the other vessels. A comparable ornamentation occurs on the amphorae from the Crimean Peninsula, from Yalta, Kerch and Proletarskaia Stanitsa,[158] and globular amphorae with a similar decoration have also been published from a seventh-century cistern on Samos[159] and the seventh-century shipwreck of Yassı Ada.[160]

Wide grooving only covers the entire vessel surface of a single amphora (No. 19), while a lighter ribbing can be found on the neck and belly of another amphora (No. 20). The ribbing most often covers the vessel's base or its lower third; on two amphorae this is combined with combed decoration on the shoulder (Nos 17–18), while in one case, it can be found on an otherwise plain amphora (No. 15).

Distribution and origins

On the testimony of the currently known finds, the late variant of LR 2 amphorae was distributed in the Aegean and the Black Sea. The distribution of LR 2B globular amphorae with a conical neck and deeply combed decoration differs from

[154] Popović 1988.

[155] Opaiţ 2004a, 12.

[156] H. Tóth – Horváth 1992, 63, 273, Fig. 16/5, Pl. 27; Vida 1999, 243; Csiky – Hárshegyi 2015, 175–176.

[157] Van Doorninck 1989, 249, Fig. 1.

[158] Якобсон 1979, 31, Рис. 13, 5–7.

[159] Hautumm 1981, Abb. 23; Karagiorgou 2001, 130, Fig. 7.1/8.

[160] Van Doorninck 1989, 249, Fig. 1/9.

that of the slightly later amphorae with combed decoration arranged in bands. The former were distributed across the Balkans,[161] while the latter are principally known from the Aegean[162] and in the coastal regions of the Black Sea,[163] although some pieces have been reported from Constantinople (Saraçhane)[164] and Italy too.[165] The type can most likely be derived from LR 2 amphorae, suggesting an Aegean origin, although there is some evidence for the type's production in North Africa and Italy.[166]

Chronology

LR 2 amphorae underwent a significant formal change in the later sixth century: while the overall form of the body and its ornamentation remained more or less unchanged, the neck became taller and the size of the cupped rim decreased.[167] The finds from Svetinja near Viminacium, assigned to the period between 567 and 596 by the excavators, stand out from among the finds of the later sixth century.[168] A high number of LR 2B amphorae were found on the Yassı Ada shipwreck, whose *post quem* date of 625/626 is based on a coin of Heraclius.[169] The LR 2C amphorae from the acropolis of Emporio on Chios are coin-dated to 640/641, to the period between the construction of the fort and its destruction in 673/674.[170] The finds from the Eupalinos Tunnel on Samos used by the Byzantines fleeing the Sasanian Persians until the Arab conquest, i.e. from the 620s to the last third of the seventh century, date from roughly the same period.[171] The current evidence

---

[161] Svetinja/Viminacium (Popović 1988, 35–37, Figs 13–14), Dobrudja: Murighiol (Opaiţ 2004a, 12), Kunszentmiklós-Bábonypuszta (H. Tóth – Horváth 1992, 63, 273, Fig. 16/5, Pl. 27; Vida 1999, 243; Csiky – Hárshegyi 2015, 175–176), for their Balkanic distribution, see Karagiorgou 2001, 131–132.

[162] Samos, cistern (Hautumm 1981, Abb. 23; Karagiorgou 2001, 130, Fig. 7.1/8), Yassı Ada, shipwreck (Van Doorninck 1989, 249, Fig. 1/9).

[163] Yalta, Kerch and Proletarskaia Stanitsa (Якобсон 1979, 31, Рис. 13, 5–7).

[164] Hayes 1992, 66, Type 10.

[165] Arthur 1989, 87; Arthur 1993, 231–244; Giardini – Murialdo 1994, 170–171; Paroli – Delogu 1993, 231–243.

[166] Piéri 1998, 100.

[167] Karagiorgou 2001, 131–132.

[168] Popović 1988, 35–37, Figs 13–14.

[169] van Doorninck 1989, 247.

[170] Ballance et al. 1989, 3, 7–8; Karagiorgou 2001, 142.

[171] Hautumm 1981, 9, 174.

thus indicates that LR 2C amphorae were quite certainly still current in the later seventh century.

The globular LR 2C amphorae with short rim, tall neck and combed decoration arranged in bands from sites on the Crimean and Taman Peninsulas and in the Don region are generally dated to a much later period, to the eighth–ninth centuries.[172] This late date is supported also by the type's occurrence in the Sarkel fort, whose *post quem* dating is 839.[173]

Catalogue

15. Amphora *(Plate 15)*
Inv. no. 3.25.73
Find context: from the Black Sea, purchase from Şükrü Gümüş, resident of Sinop (Tersane cd.)
Orange (5 YR 6/6) amphora tempered with fine-grained mixed sand; hard surface, clear ringing tone when tapped. Short, strongly everted, thickened, semi-circular-sectioned rim; downward widening conical neck; globular body with rounded base, without an indication of a basal knob. The curved, oval-sectioned handles spring from the upper third of the neck to above the shoulder. The body is covered with ribbing from the lower handle attachment to the lower vessel third. There is a semi-circular groove incised before firing above one of the lower handle attachments and an X-shaped incision, also made before firing, on the opposite side.
H. 49.5 cm, rim diam. 7.4 cm (ext.), 5.4 cm (int.), rim H. 0.8 cm, rim Th. 1 cm, neck diam. 6.6–10 cm, neck H. 10 cm, belly diam. 39.47 cm Th. 0.45 cm, left handle H. 15.2 cm (ext.), 10.8 cm (int.), left handle W. 3.6 cm, left handle Th. 2.7 cm, right handle H. 14.5 cm (ext.), 10.3 cm (int.), right handle W. 3.5 cm, right handle Th. 2.6 cm, rib W. 2 cm, X motif L. 5.5 cm, X motif W. 4.2 cm, semi-circular groove W. 4.8 cm

16. Amphora *(Plate 16)*
Inv. no. 4.2.83
Find context: from the Black Sea, purchase from Durmuş Semiz
Bright yellowish-brown (10 YR 6/6) amphora tempered with fine-grained mixed sand; hard fabric, clear ringing tone when tapped. Short, slightly funnel-shaped, rounded, slightly thickened, everted rim; downward widening conical neck; flattened globular body with the greatest diameter in the upper third; rounded base with no indication of a basal knob. The long, curved, oval-sectioned handles spring from the upper third of the neck to the greatest diameter. Three wide parallel bands of lightly combed grooves cover

[172] Якобсон 1979, 31, Рис. 13, 5–8, 32.
[173] Плетнева 1959, 243, Рис. 29/5, 244.

the body under the lower handle attachment. The vessel body is smooth, without ribbing, but the base is lightly ribbed.
H. 50.5 cm, d: 39.47 cm, rim diam. 8.3–8.6 cm (ext.), 6.5 cm (int.), rim Th. 1 cm, neck diam. 7.5–12 cm, neck H. 10 cm, left handle H. 14.4 cm (ext.), 9.7 cm (int.), left handle W. 3.8 cm, left handle Th. 2.4 cm, right handle H. 14.8 cm (ext.), 10.6 cm (int.), right handle W. 3.9 cm, right handle Th. 2.5 cm, W. of combed grooves 0.8 cm, decorated band W. 6.7 cm

17. Amphora *(Plate 17)*
Inv. no. 6.1.83
Find context: from the Black Sea, purchase from fisherman Ömer Saral
Orange (7.5 YR 6/6) amphora tempered with fine-grained mixed sand; hard surface, clear ringing tone when tapped. Slightly everted, strongly thickened, rounded rim; downward widening conical neck; flattened globular body with the greatest circumference in the upper third. The curved, oval-sectioned handles spring from the upper third of the neck to above the shoulder. The neck is gently ribbed. There are two parallel bands of light combing under the lower handle attachment, around the vessel's greatest diameter, which is also visible at the lower handle attachment. The lowermost part of the body is decorated with widely spaced ribbing of shallow grooves, the vessel base has deeper grooves.
H. 57.5 cm, d: 39.15 cm, rim diam. 8.5 cm (ext.), 6 cm (int.), rim Th. 1.4 cm, neck diam. 7.8–12.4 cm, neck H. 11.8 cm, left handle H. 15 cm (ext.), 9.7 cm (int.), left handle W. 3.7 cm, left handle Th. 2.5 cm, right handle H. 15.5 cm (ext.), 10.7 cm (int.), right handle W. 3.7 cm, right handle Th. 2.6 cm, W. of combed grooves 1 cm, decorated band W. 4.2 cm (body), 2.5 cm (base)

18. Amphora *(Plate 18)*
Inv. no. 10.11.1981
Find context: from the Black Sea, purchase from fisherman Mustafa Arslan
Dull yellowish-orange (10 YR 6/4) amphora tempered with fine-grained mixed sand; hard fabric, clear ringing tone when tapped. Short, ring-like thickened rim; downward-widening conical neck; globular body with the greatest diameter in the upper third; rounded base with no indication of a knob. The curved, oval-sectioned handles spring from the upper third of the neck to above the shoulder. Four bands of combed decoration cover the vessel body from the lower end of the neck (W. 0.9 cm, the uppermost band begins 3 cm underneath the neck, the lowermost band encircles the greatest diameter). The lower half of the vessel body is covered with widely spaced ribbing with light grooves in-between that continues on the vessel base. Finger-nail impressions made before firing can be seen on the shoulder.
H. 51 cm, d: 39.47 cm, rim diam. 8.3 cm (ext.), 6.3 cm (int.), rim H. 0.7 cm, rim Th. 1.1 cm, neck diam. 7.3–12.2 cm, neck H. 10.7 cm, left handle H. 15.5 cm (ext.), 9.5 cm (int.), left handle W. 3.9 cm, left handle Th. 2.7 cm, right handle H. 15.4 cm (ext.), 10.4 cm

(int.), right handle W. 4 cm, right handle Th. 2.7 cm, combed decoration W. 8.3 cm, rib W. 3.4 cm, lower rib W. 1.1 cm

19. Amphora *(Plate 19)*
Inv. no. 10.12.1981
Find context: from the Black Sea, purchase from fisherman Mustafa Arslan
Bright yellowish-brown (10 YR 6/6) amphora tempered with fine-grained mixed sand; hard surface, clear ringing tone when tapped. Short, slightly everted, rounded rim; tall, downward strongly widening neck; globular body with the greatest diameter in the upper third, the sides are wholly rounded. The long, curved, oval-sectioned handles covered with barely prominent ribbing down the centre spring from the upper third of the neck under the rim to the above the shoulder. The vessel body is covered with widely spaced ribbing with wide, shallow, rounded grooves in-between from the lower handle attachment to the lower third of the vessel body. An incised motif of two triangles set with the tips towards each other can be seen on the shoulder above the ribbing.
H. 57 cm, diam. 39.15 cm, rim diam. 7.8 cm (ext.), 5.2 cm (int.), rim Th. 1.2 cm, neck diam. 7.4–13 cm, neck H. 10.3 cm, left handle H. 15.6 cm (ext.), 10 cm (int.), left handle W. 4 cm, left handle Th. 2.2 cm, right handle H. 15.3 cm (ext.), 10.5 cm (int.), right handle W. 3.8 cm, right handle W. 2.5 cm, rib W. 1–2 cm, incision W. 4.4 cm, incision L. 5.8 cm

20. Amphora *(Plate 20)*
Inv. no. 28.4.80
Find context: from the Black Sea, purchase from Fahrettin Türe, resident of Sinop (found in an area administered by the Forest Management Office, *Orman İşletmesi*)
Yellowish-orange (7.5 YR 7/8) amphora tempered with fine-grained mixed sand; hard surface, dull tone when tapped. Slightly everted, thickened rim with a rib around the rim interior; downward widening conical neck with ribbing on the exterior (six ribs); globular body with rounded base and no indication of a basal knob. The short, curved, oval-sectioned handles spring from the upper third of the neck under the rim, the exterior more curved than the interior surface. An 11 cm wide band of double lines spaced 0.9 cm apart covers the body from the lower handle attachment to the greatest diameter.
H. 55.5 cm, rim diam. 8 cm (ext.), 6 cm (int.), rim Th. 1.1 cm, neck diam. 7.1–11 cm, neck H. 11 cm, left handle H. 14 cm (ext.), 9 cm (int.), left handle W. 3.5 cm, left handle Th. 2 cm, right handle H. 13.4 cm (ext.), 8.5 cm (int.), right handle W. 3.5 cm, right handle Th. 1.8 cm, Th. 0.75 cm

21. Amphora *(Plate 21)*
Inv. no. 36.4.77
Find context: from the Black Sea, purchase from İbrahim Önder, resident of Sinop (Sakarya cd.)

Orange (7.5 YR 6/6) amphora tempered with fine-grained mixed sand, hard surface, clear ringing tone when tapped. Slightly thickened, rounded rim; downward widening conical neck; flattened globular body with the greatest diameter in the upper third; rounded base with a flat disc-shaped knob in the centre of the base. The body is covered with narrowly spaced, but occasionally interrupted combed decoration from the lower handle attachment to the greatest diameter. The lower half of the vessel body has barely prominent ribbing with wide, shallow grooves in-between. The neck is also lightly ribbed. The vessel base is smooth.

H. 51 cm, diam. 39.31 cm, diam. 8.4 cm (ext.), 5.7 cm (int.), rim Th. 1.2 cm, neck diam. 7.7–12.5 cm, neck H. 10 cm, left handle H. 14.7 cm (ext.), 9.9 cm (int.), left handle W. 3.4 cm, left handle Th. 2.5 cm, right handle H. 4.7 cm (ext.), 9.8 cm (int.), right handle W. 3.8 cm, right handle Th. 2.4 cm, density of combing 1 mm, decorated band W. 13.5 cm, rib W. 2.3 cm, knob diam. 2 cm

Crimean (Black Sea) amphorae

Research history

Major advances have been made in the research on eighth–ninth-century amphorae found on the northern Black Sea coast since the 1930s. This class of material first received scholarly attention when Mikhail I. Artamonov assessed the ceramic finds from the Tsimliansk fort (*городище*) that was later identified with Sarkel. He noted that the amphorae were ribbed cylindrical vessels with relatively tall neck and rounded base fired to a red colour. The number of amphora fragments suggested that these vessels did not play a particularly important role in the settlement's life. Artamonov cited parallels from the Don and Volga regions as well as from various sites of the Saltovo-Maiak culture such as the eponymous Verkhne-Saltovo and Maiatskoe gorodishche settlements, although he emphasised that while the amphorae from Saltovo were ribbed, the ones from Tsimliansk also included pieces with combed decoration. In his view, the amphorae were local products and not imports, despite their resemblance to late antique (in Artamonov's words, late Roman) forms.[174]

The eighth–ninth-century "ovoid" amphorae termed the Saltovo type continued to be associated with the Saltovo-Maiak culture in the 1950s, although Iakobson, who wrote a comprehensive study on medieval amphorae, derived these vessels from the earlier late antique LR 1 type. He assumed a local production in view of the pottery kilns uncovered on the Saltovo settlement and dated the amphorae to

---

[174] Артамонов 1935, 67–72.

the ninth century in view of their stratigraphic context and the associated finds. He pointed out that these amphorae were rare in Byzantium and were distributed on the northern coast of the Black Sea.[175]

In her assessment of the amphora finds from the Sarkel settlement, Pletneva too assigned the vessels to Group (*вид*) 1 of amphorae and highlighted their association with LR 1 amphorae. In line with the findings of Iakobson's excavations, she too located their workshops to the northern coast of the Black Sea, to the Crimean Peninsula. Similar amphorae were generally dated to the eighth–ninth centuries and their distribution extended from the Upper Donets region to the Kuban region. They were typical finds of the ninth–tenth-century Khazar-period occupation level of the Sarkel settlement.[176] Drawing from the findings of petrographic analyses, Pletneva also compared the fabric of the amphorae with that of the pottery from Tmutarakan and noted that the use of clay types typical for later periods began at this time.[177]

Iakobson can be credited with the still best overview of eighth–ninth-century amphorae. In addition to an excellent formal analysis and chronological classification of these vessels, he also uncovered amphora kilns at Chaban-kule, Kanakskaia balka and Karantinnaia bukhta in the eastern part of the Crimean Peninsula. According to him, three main amphora types can be distinguished. Variant 1 is a large, 60–70 cm tall amphora fired to a red colour with widening straight rim, tall neck, ribbed or grooved angular handles, long, tapering and lightly ribbed body and rounded base. These vessels were distributed in the western part of Taurike and the eastern Crimea, the Don region and the northern Donets region as far as Saltovo, although they are also attested on Slavic settlements in the Middle Don region (Romeno-Borshevo culture).[178] Variant 2 is a slightly smaller, 40–45 cm tall amphora with cylindrical rim, shorter neck and oval, prominently ribbed body. These vessels were produced in the kilns uncovered at Kanakskaia balka and were distributed in the eastern part of the Crimean Peninsula, on the Kerch Peninsula, as well as in the Sea of Azov and the Don region (Sarkel).[179]

In 2001, Parshina, Teslenko and Zelenko published a comprehensive overview of the production of these amphorae on the Crimean Peninsula, in which they discussed all the known eighth–tenth-century ceramic workshop finds,

---

[175] Якобсон 1951, 330–334.
[176] Плетнева 1959, 241–244.
[177] Плетнева 1963, 50–53, Рис. 32.
[178] Якобсон 1979, 29–31.
[179] Якобсон 1979, 31.

principally the kilns. According to their survey, there were pottery workshops by the dozen from modern Feodosia to Sevastopol, i.e. from one-time Kaffa (Kefe) to Byzantine Chersonesus on the southern coast of the Crimean Peninsula.[180]

The amphorae found among the early medieval finds from the occupation levels of Taman gorodishche were discussed by Viktor I. Chkhaidze, who argued that these vessels indicated the continuity of late antique forms. These ovoid, less prominently ribbed amphorae were generally designated as local (*туземный*) or Saltovo vessels;[181] later, following Iakobson's work, they became known as Black Sea (*причерноморские*) amphorae.

Chkhaidze distinguished two main types among the amphorae from the Khazar occupation levels of Tmutarakan (Tamatarkha). Type 1 represented amphorae with grooved body from the second quarter of the sixth century and the mid-seventh century, which survived as late as the later ninth century. He identified several sub-variants:

(A) Amphorae with oval rim and handles springing from the rim, made from clay tempered with limestone and grog, fired to a purplish-red colour. This variant can be dated to the 570–580s, although pieces from Constantinople and Chersonesus attest to their use up to the tenth century;

(B) Amphorae with widening rim, made from clay tempered with limestone and grog, fired to an orange colour, covered with a greenish-white slip. The earliest vessels come from the second quarter of the sixth century. Their use is attested between the late sixth and later ninth centuries on the Crimean Peninsula;

(V) Spindle-shaped amphorae made from clay tempered with limestone and grog, fired to a brick red colour, covered with a light slip. These amphorae were distributed in Serbia, Bulgaria, Syria, Palestine and the Crimea from the later sixth century to the seventh–eighth centuries, and up to the later ninth century in some regions. These amphorae were produced in Chersonesus;

(G) Amphorae with everted, cylindrical rim, used from the earlier ninth century to the early eleventh century, produced in Soter urochishche;

(D) Amphorae with straight-cut rim, made from clay tempered with coarse-grained grog and carbonates, fired to a yellow or brick-red colour, covered with a red slip. The earliest exemplars of this variant appear in the later seventh century, with their use spanning the period between the later eighth century to the early eleventh century. They were produced in Chersonesus near Radiogorka, as well as in Kanakskaia balka and Soter urochishche;

---

[180] Паршина – Тесленко – Зеленко 2001, 53–79.

[181] Ляпушкин 1941, 208, 227.

(E) Conical amphorae stamped with a cross in a small circle on the neck, dating from the earlier tenth century.[182]

Fabric and temper

The fabric and temper of the amphorae assigned to this type vary and several groups can be distinguished among them. The fabric of two amphorae (Nos 28, 32) is clay tempered with fine pyroxene, resembling the classical LR 1 vessels. However, a fabric with a fine-grained mixed sand temper was more typical (No. 24), sometimes combined with mica (Nos 27, 29) and grog (No. 31). There were also amphorae tempered with coarser, more large-grained tempering agents, most of which were generally tempered solely with coarse grog (Nos 23, 26, 30), while one piece was tempered with large-grained sand in addition to the coarse grog (No. 25).

Similarly to the tempering agents, the colour of the amphorae too varies, although there is no apparent correlation between colour and tempering agent. Amphorae tempered with pyroxene were generally fired to a yellowish-red colour (5 YR 5/6, 7.5 YR7/6), while pieces tempered with grog are slightly darker, ranging from reddish-yellow to orange, between 5 YR 6/6–7/8 on the Munsell scale. The amphorae tempered with fine-grained sand and mica were fired to reddish-yellow and brown hues (5 YR 6/8, 5 YR7/8 and 10 YR6/2, 10 YR 7/4). Neither was slipped, although this can most likely be explained by their find contexts (all were recovered from the sea).

A look at the tempering agents used during the production of the parallels to the amphorae reveals a similar diversity. Pletneva distinguished seven different tempers in the fabric of the Saltovo amphorae dated to the eighth–ninth centuries from Tmutarakan on the Taman Peninsula: (1) well-levigated red clay, (2) grog and quartzite, (3) pyroxene, (4) a loose, crumbly fabric tempered with grog, feldspar, quartzite, carbonate and pyroxene, (5) well-levigated, without sand, (6) fine-grained sand temper, and (7) well-levigated clay with calcite. She found that these fabrics and tempers were also used in later periods, in the tenth–eleventh centuries.[183]

Chkhaidze distinguished amphorae tempered with limestone and grog fired to a purplish-red colour (A) and amphorae tempered with limestone and grog fired to an orange colour and covered with a greenish-white slip (B) at Tmutarakan.

---

[182] Чхаидзе 2008, 145–152.
[183] Плетнева 1963, 50–53, Рис. 32.

He claimed that the amphorae of fabric A were produced in the southern part of the Crimean Peninsula, at Chaban-Kule, Kanakskaia Balka, Soter and in other workshops, while the amphorae of fabric B dated from the late sixth century to the later ninth century. Of the other types distinguished by Chkhaidze, Type V, tempered with limestone and grog, fired to a brick red colour and covered with a light slip, was produced in Chersonesus, while Type D, tempered with large pieces of grog and carbonate, fired to a yellow or brick red colour and covered with a red slip, whose use spanned the period from the later seventh to the early eleventh century, was produced in Chersonesus near Radiogorka, as well as in the workshops at Kanakskaia balka and Soter urochishche.[184]

Form and dimensions

In terms of its form, the main traits of this amphora conform to those of the late antique LR 1 amphorae, although several differences can be noted. The rim is short, slightly everted and rounded (Nos 23, 26–29, 31) or strongly everted and flat (Nos 24–25, 30, 32). The neck is short and conical or, in some cases, tall and cylindrical (Nos 24, 26, 31–32), and rarely decorated with ribbing (Nos 24–26, 30–31). The amphorae have a cylindrical, barrel-shaped body with wide shoulders and the body tapers slightly towards the base. The shoulders are curved, a slight transition can be noted between the body and the base, the base is rounded and lacks a knob. The handles spring from under the rim and curve to the shoulder. They are oval-sectioned and have a shallow groove down the centre (Nos 23–25, 27–28, 30–32), although in many cases they lack a groove. There is a drop-shaped impression at the lower handle attachment on one amphora (No. 24). Based on their rim, shape and decoration Crimean amphorae can be divided into two separate variants: variant 1 is characterised by its triangular rim, oval body and shallow grooves, while amphorae belonging to variant 2 are usually narrower and the grooves are deeper, while their rims are rounded and slightly everted.

The height of Crimean amphorae varies significantly. The smallest exemplars are around 40 cm tall (38–41 cm: Nos 27–29), with the average height being *ca.* 45 cm (44.5–46 cm: 23, 25–26, 30–32); the tallest amphora is 49.5 cm high (No. 24). The greatest diameter of the amphora body shows a similar distribution, with three major size ranges: 20–22 cm (Nos 28, 30–32), 24–25 cm (Nos 23, 25–26, 29), and 32.15 cm (No. 24). There seems to be some correlation between

[184] Чхаидзе 2008, 147–151.

the two sizes: the largest and smallest values were measured on the same vessels, although the proportions are not unchanged.

All Crimean amphorae have a narrow rim, a relatively uniform trait. The exterior diameter ranges between 6 and 9.5 cm, the interior one between 4 and 7.3 cm. The neck is short (4.3–9.9 cm) and generally has a downward flaring conical form, with an upper diameter of 4.9–7.1 cm and a lower diameter of 9.1–10.2 cm.

Ornamentation

Crimean amphorae are generally covered with ribbing with shallow grooves in-between; the ribbing is less pronounced than on LR 1 amphorae, but generally covers the entire body. There are eight ribbed amphorae in the assemblage (Nos 23, 26–32), while two vessels lack ribbing on their body (Nos 24–25). There were no visible remnants of a slip on the vessel surfaces, but this may be due to their find contexts.

Origins and distribution

The amphorae in question were principally distributed along the northern Black Sea coast, including the Crimean[185] and Taman Peninsulas (Tmutarakan),[186] as well as in the Don region (Sarkel),[187] along the southern Black Sea coast (Sinop), in Constantinople[188] and in the Aegean (Bozburun)[189] (*Map 2*). The kilns of the workshops producing these vessels were identified fairly early, in 1925, by Barsamov in the southern part of the Crimean Peninsula,[190] followed by the excavations conducted by Iakobson in 1952–53 at Chaban-kule and at Kanakskaia balka.[191] Amphora kilns have also been uncovered near Chersonesus in Karantinnaia bukhta (bay) and near Radiogorka.[192] A full list of workshop sites has been assembled by Parshina, Teslenko and Zelenko.[193]

[185] Якобсон 1979, 29–31.

[186] Плетнева 1963, 50–53, Рис. 32; Чхаидзе 2008, 145–146.

[187] Артамонов 1935, 67–72; Плетнева 1959, 241–244.

[188] Günsenin 2012, 157–164; Denker et al. 2013, 205–208.

[189] Hocker 1998, 3–13; Kingsley 2009, 35; http://nauticalarch.org/projects/bozburun-byzantine-shipwreck-excavation/ (last accessed March 9, 2016).

[190] Барсамов 1926, 185.

[191] Якобсон 1979, 29–31; Чхаидзе 2008, 147–148.

[192] Чхаидзе 2008, 149, 151.

[193] Паршина – Тесленко – Зеленко 2001, 53–79.

Chronology

Russian scholars generally date Crimean amphorae to the eighth–ninth centuries on the testimony of their find contexts. They abound on the settlements of the Saltovo-Maiak culture and their chronological position is generally adjusted to the culture's chronology. While the use of these amphorae began in the late seventh century on the Crimean Peninsula, they only became widespread in the Don region during the ninth century.

Catalogue

Variant 1

22. Amphora *(Plate 22)*
Inv. no. 3.4.012
Find context: from the Black Sea at Ayancık, purchase from Şükrü Özdemir (March 6, 2012)
Reddish-yellow (5 YR 6/6) amphora tempered with coarse-grained sand; hard fabric, ringing tone when tapped. Strongly everted, thickened rim with a groove around the rim interior; tall, conical, smooth neck; oval, downward tapering body with the greatest diameter in the upper third, but no transitions; smooth, rounded base. The curved, oval-sectioned handles with a pair of shallow grooves down the centre spring from the upper third of the neck to above the shoulder. The vessel body is covered with widely spaced light ribbing with extremely shallow grooves in-between, creating a rippled surface.
H. 47.5 cm, diam. 29.9 cm, rim diam. 7.6 cm (ext.), 5.3 cm (int.), rim H. 1.2 cm, rim Th. 1.3 cm, neck diam. 5.7–7.8 cm, neck H. 7.4 cm, left handle H. 11.8 cm (ext.), 8.1 cm (int.), left handle W. 3.4 cm, left handle Th. 2,2 cm, right handle H. 11 cm (ext.), 7.9 cm (int.), right handle W. 3.4 cm, right handle Th. 1.8 cm, rib W. 1.8 cm

23. Amphora *(Plate 23)*
Inv. no. 4.5.82
Find context: purchase from Ali Arslan, village of Kuşluca, Trabzon (November 24, 1982)
Reddish-yellow (5 YR 6/8) amphora tempered with coarse-grained grog; hard fabric, dull tone when tapped. Everted, funnel-like, rounded rim; tall, strongly downward widening neck; barrel-shaped, tapering body with rounded, smooth base. The curved, oval-sectioned handles, each with a shallow groove down the centre, spring from the middle part of the neck to above the shoulder, the right handle is more angular. The lower half of the body is covered with widely spaced ribbing with slender, shallow grooves in-between.
H. 46 cm, diam. 25.25 cm, rim diam. 8.2–7.1 cm (ext.), 4.2–5.7 cm (int.), rim H. 1.7 cm, rim Th. 1.2 cm, neck diam. 5.8–11.4 cm, neck H. 8.8 cm, left handle H. 12 cm (ext.),

6.4 cm (int.), left handle W. 3.5 cm, left handle Th. 2.4 cm, right handle H. 11 cm (ext.), 5.7 cm (int.), right handle W. 3.3 cm, right handle Th. 2.1 cm, rib W. 1.6 cm

24. Amphora *(Plate 24)*
Inv. no. 7.2.90
Find context: from the Black Sea, marine department of the police headquarters (*Emniyet Müdürlüğü Deniz Şubesi*)
Light brownish-grey (10 YR 6/2) amphora tempered with fine-grained sand; hard fabric, dull tone when tapped. Strongly everted, triangular-sectioned rim, one section is flat with a groove in its centre; cylindrical neck with three prominent ribs; oval body with the greatest diameter in the upper third, and a transition above the base; smooth, rounded base with an indent. The curved, oval-sectioned handles with a shallow groove down the centre spring from the middle of the neck to above the shoulder. There is a drop-shaped impression at the lower handle attachment. The vessel body is smooth without ribbing, save for the rippled surface produced by the wheel-turning.
H. 49.5 cm, diam. 32.15 cm, rim diam. 8.7 cm (ext.), 6.1 cm (int.), rim H. 1.2 cm, rim Th. 1.3 cm, neck diam. 6.9–9.1 cm, neck H. 8.8 cm, left handle H. 12 cm (ext.), 6.6 cm (int.), left handle W. 3.8 cm, left handle Th. 2.4 cm, right handle H. 12.6 cm (ext.), 6.4 cm (int.), right handle W. 4 cm, right handle Th. 2.5 cm

25. Amphora *(Plate 25)*
Inv. no. 9.3.1981
Reg. no. 2350
Find context: purchase from Saim Arslan (December 8, 1981)
Orange (5 YR 6/6) amphora tempered with coarse-grained sand and grog as well as a little mica; hard fabric, dull tone when tapped. Strongly everted, thickened, triangular-sectioned rim with a light groove around the flattened top; tall, slightly widening conical neck with four barely prominent ribs; barrel-shaped body with rounded shoulders and base, the lower part tapers slightly into a conical form. The angular, oval-sectioned handles, each with a pair of shallow grooves down the centre, spring from the middle of the neck to the shoulder. The body is smooth, save for an incised spiralling decoration of seven incised lines and a pair of shallow grooves above the base.
H. 45.5 cm, diam. 25.94 cm, rim diam. 7.7 cm (ext.), 5.6 cm (int.), rim H. 0.9 cm, rim Th. 1 cm, neck diam. 6.15–10.2 cm, neck H. 8.7 cm, left handle H. 14 cm (ext.), 7.8 cm (int.), left handle W. 3.1 cm, left handle Th. 2.4 cm, right handle H. 13.2 cm (ext.), 8.2 cm (int.), right handle W. 3 cm, right handle Th. 2.3 cm, incised line W. 0.15 cm, incised line spacing 0.8 cm

Variant 2

26. Amphora *(Plate 26)*
Inv. no. 2.2.83
Find context: purchase from Ali Arslan, resident of the village of Kuşluca, Trabzon (September 7, 1983)
Dull orange (5 YR 7/4) amphora tempered with coarse-grained grog; hard fabric, dull tone when tapped; lacking one handle. Slightly everted, rounded rim; cylindrical neck with triple triangular-sectioned ribs; barrel-shaped, tapering body. The angular, oval-sectioned handle springs from under the rim to the shoulder. The handle is not grooved and has an oval indent at the lower attachment. The body is covered with widely spaced ribs; the grooving between the ribs is shallow on the upper vessel part and deeper above the base. The grooving ends in a spiral on the vessel base.
H. 46 cm, diam. 24.2 cm, rim diam. 7.4 cm (ext.), 5.5 cm (int.), rim Th. 1.1 cm, neck H. 6.3 cm, neck diam. 6.6–7.8 cm, left handle H. 10.5 cm (ext.), 5.8 cm (int.), left handle W. 3.15 cm, left handle Th. 2.2 cm, rib W. 1.5 cm (shoulder), 2 cm (belly), 1.7 cm (base).

27. Amphora *(Plate 27)*
Inv. no. 6.1.73
Reg. no. 1705
Find context: purchase from fisherman Şükrü Gümüş, resident of Sinop
Pale brown (10 YR 7/4), thin-walled amphora tempered with fine-grained sand and mica; hard fabric. Everted, rounded rim, conical neck. Almost cylindrical body with oval upper part and conical lower part, with the greatest diameter in the upper third. The vessel body does not taper at the transition above the base. The angular, flat, oval-sectioned handles spring from under the rim to the shoulder. The upper handle attachment is set immediately below the rim. The right handle has a double rib, the left handle a single rib, and there is a shallow groove on the right handle at the lower attachment. The body is covered with widely spaced ribbing with shallow, wide grooves in-between from the neck downward. The grooving continues down the base, which is smooth. A hard, black, pitch-like residue covers the rim interior.
H. 38 cm, diam. 23.08 cm, rim diam. 6.5 cm (ext.), 4.3 cm (int.), rim H. 1.3 cm, rim Th. 1 cm, neck diam. 5.5 cm, neck H. 4.3 cm, left handle H. 9.5 cm (ext.), 6.2 cm (int.), left handle W. 3.3 cm, left handle Th. 1.8 cm, right handle H. 10 cm (ext.), 6.7 cm (int.), right handle W. 3.2 cm, right handle Th. 1.7 cm, diam. of groove on right handle lower attachment 3.4 cm x 2 cm, rib W. 1.5–2 cm

28. Amphora *(Plate 28)*
Inv. no. 10.03.99
Reg. no. 3275
Find context: from the Black Sea, purchase from fisherman Mustafa Kaymak, resident of Sinop (Camikebir Mahallesi, Alan sokak 7) (June 7, 1999)
Reddish-yellow (7.5 YR 7/6) amphora tempered with fine-grained pyroxene, covered with a light coloured (originally perhaps white) slip; hard fabric, clear ringing tone when tapped. Slightly everted, rounded rim; narrow, downward widening conical neck; barrel-shaped, slightly tapering body with rounded base and a slightly prominent semi-spherical knob in the centre of the base. The curved, oval-sectioned handles, each with a pair of shallow grooves down the centre, spring from immediately under the rim to the shoulder. The body is covered with ribbing with extremely shallow grooves in-between from the neck downward, more narrowly spaced on the shoulder and more widely spaced on the belly. The base is smooth, without ribbing.
H. 39.5 cm, diam. 20.37 cm, rim diam. 5.9–6.1 cm (ext.), 4 cm (int.), rim Th. 1.1 cm, neck diam. 4.9–7.7 cm, neck H. 6.3 cm, left handle H. 9.6 cm (ext.), 6.6 cm (int.), left handle W. 3 cm, left handle Th. 1.7 cm, right handle H. 9.5 cm (ext.), 6.7 cm (int.), right handle W. 3.1 cm, right handle Th. 1.6 cm, rib W. 0.6 cm (shoulder), 1.3 cm (belly), 0.8 cm (base), knob diam. 2.3 cm

29. Amphora *(Plate 29)*
Inv. no. 11.2.83
Reg. no. 2595
Find context: purchase from Tayfun Güner, resident of Sinop (July 6, 1983)
Reddish-yellow (5 YR 6/8), well-fired amphora tempered with fine-grained sand and little mica; clear ringing tone when tapped. Slightly everted, rounded rim; short, conical neck; the upper body is oval, the lower body is conical with rounded base. The flat, slightly curved, angular, oval-sectioned handles spring from directly under the rim to the shoulder. The body is ribbed with shallow, wide grooves in-between from the neck downward, the relatively wide ribs cover the body down to the body-base transition.
H. 41 cm, diam. 25.62 cm, rim diam. 9.5 cm (ext.), 7.3 cm (int.), rim Th. 1.2 cm, neck diam. 7.1 cm, neck H. 5.2 cm, left handle H. 11.5 cm (ext.), 7.7 cm (ext.), left handle W. 3.6 cm, left handle Th. 2 cm, right handle H. 11.8 cm (ext.), 8 cm (ext.), right handle W. 3.6 cm, right handle Th. 1.8 cm, rib W. 1.4 cm

30. Amphora *(Plate 30)*
Inv. no. 22.4.84
Find context: from the Black Sea, purchase from Nurettin Zarflıoğlu
Reddish-yellow (5 YR 7/6) amphora tempered with coarse-grained grog; hard surface, clear ringing tone when tapped. Short, strongly everted, triangular-sectioned rim with flat surface; relatively tall, slightly downward widening conical neck with three barely

prominent ribs, two more narrowly spaced ribs on the lower part; barrel-shaped, slightly tapering body with conical middle section and rounded, smooth base. The arched, oval-sectioned handles, each with a wide groove down the centre, spring from under the rim to the shoulder. The vessel body is relatively smooth: instead of ribbing, the very shallow grooves create a slightly rippled surface.
H. 46 cm, diam. 71.5 cm, rim diam. 7.2 cm (ext.), 4.2 cm (int.), rim H. 1 cm, rim Th. 1 cm, neck diam. 5.8–8.4 cm, neck H. 8.4 cm, left handle H. 12.2 cm (ext.), 7.7 cm (int.), left handle W. 3.6 cm, left handle Th. 2.2 cm, right handle H. 12 cm (ext.), 7.2 cm (int.), right handle W. 3.6 cm, right handle Th. 2.2 cm, rib W. 1.6 cm

31. Amphora *(Plate 31)*
Inv. no. 36.7.80
Find context: from the Black Sea, purchase from Mustafa Arslan
Reddish-yellow amphora (5 YR 7/8) tempered with fine-grained sand and some fine-grained grog; hard fabric, clear ringing tone when tapped. Short, curved, everted rim; relatively tall, cylindrical neck with triple ribbing; barrel-shaped, cylindrical body with rounded, smooth base. The angular, oval-sectioned handles, each with very shallow grooving, spring from under the rim to the shoulder. Part of the neck is covered with iron oxide residue, the shoulder is ribbed underneath it. The body is relatively smooth with very shallow grooving in-between, creating a slightly rippled surface.
H. 46 cm, diam. 69.5 cm, rim diam. 7.9–8.2 cm (ext.), 5.9 cm (int.), rim Th. 0.9 cm, neck diam. 6.6–8.5 cm, neck H. 6.3 cm, rib W. 1.2 cm, left handle H. 11.4 cm (ext.), 6.6 cm (int.), left handle W. 3.1 cm, left handle Th. 2.2 cm, right handle H. 11.9 cm (ext.), 7.2 cm (int.), right handle W. 2.9 cm, handle Th. 1.9 cm, rib W. 2 cm

32. Amphora *(Plate 32)*
Inv. no. 6.1.89
Reg. no. 2927
Find context: from the shipwreck found near Karakum, donated by the High School for Water Management (September 22, 1989)
Yellowish-red (5 YR 5/6) amphora tempered with fine-grained pyroxene, covered with a white residue (perhaps ash) and black burnt patches; hard fabric, clear ringing tone when tapped. The rim, side and base are deformed and indented. Short, angular, lozenge-sectioned, everted rim with a groove around the rim interior; tall, cylindrical neck; barrel-shaped body with cylindrical mid-section and rounded base with a small, flat, hemispherical knob in the centre that is secondarily deformed and indented. The angular, oval-sectioned handles, each with a deep, wide groove, spring from under the rim to the shoulder. The body is ribbed from the lower handle attachment downward: narrowly spaced ribs with deep grooves in-between on the shoulder, widely spaced ribs with shallow grooves in-between on the belly, and more pronounced ribbing on the base.

H. 44.5 cm, diam. 20.7 cm, rim diam. 6.7 cm (ext.), 5.2 cm (int.), rim H. 1.5 cm, rim Th. 1.1 cm, neck diam. 6–7.5 cm, neck H. 9.9 cm, left handle H. 12.6 cm (ext.), 8.6 cm (int.), left handle W. 3.4 cm, left handle Th. 2.2 cm, right handle H. 12.5 cm (ext.), 8.6 cm (int.), right handle W. 3.2 cm, right handle Th. 2.2 cm, rib W. 0.5 cm (shoulder), 2.2 cm (belly), 0.8 cm (base), knob diam. 1.2 cm

Medieval transport vessels

A standardisation of amphorae can be noted from the late ninth and the tenth century, suggesting that most of these transport vessels were the products of a larger workshop area, a contention confirmed by petrographic studies that indicated that there were no major changes in the fabric of the amphorae between the tenth and thirteenth centuries.[194] The collection of the Sinop Archaeological Museum occupies a prominent place in amphora studies: the tenth- to thirteenth-century amphorae studied by Nergis Günsenin in the 1980s became one of the foundations for the typological classification of medieval Byzantine amphorae. It must here be noted that Günsenin did not cover the tall-necked, flat-handled vessels known also as Tmutarakan-type jugs, of which there is an impressive number in the museum's collection.

Günsenin 1 (*Ganos*) amphorae

The amphorae assigned to this type were made from clay tempered with fine-grained sand and mica fired to a yellow or orange colour. The amphorae have a slightly thickened, rounded rim, a short neck and a pear-shaped, strongly tapering body. Günsenin 1 amphorae have short, slightly arched, oval-sectioned handles springing from the middle of the neck to the shoulder. One distinctive feature is the ribbing covering the entire body and the frequent presence of graffiti incised after firing.

Research history

Russian research in the northern Black Sea region soon took note of the pear-shaped amphorae with grooved body since these occurred in abundance on all tenth–eleventh-century sites of the Crimean and Taman Peninsulas as well as in the Don region. In the first comprehensive treatment of the medieval amphorae of the northern Black Sea coast, Iakobson too noted the standardisation of amphora types from the later ninth and the tenth centuries, which he explained by their production in larger workshops along the Black Sea. He cited short-necked, tapering, round-based amphorae from occupation levels uncovered at Chersonesus dated to the later ninth and the tenth century by coins of Basileus I (867–886) and Basileus II (976–1025), quoting comparable amphorae from

[194] Плетнева 1963, 53; Булгаков – Яковлев 2003.

the Khazar-period occupation levels of Sarkel and the Mangana quarter of Constantinople.[195] According to his descriptions, the stamps – among which he distinguished twelve types – often occurring on the handles of this amphora type were also documented among the finds from Chersonesus and Sarkel. Similar amphorae were often found together with tall-necked, flat-handled jugs.[196]

In her assessment of the ceramics from Sarkel, Pletneva assigned the short-necked, strongly grooved amphorae with wide pear-shaped body to her Type 3, which she dated to the close of the tenth and the early eleventh century. In her view, these amphorae were produced in the Black Sea region, although she also distinguished a local variant, probably produced in Sarkel, on the basis of the fabric (chaff-tempered vessels fired to a dark red colour).[197] In her discussion of the amphorae from Tmutarakan, Pletneva compared the results of the petrographic analyses performed in the laboratory of O. Iu. Krug with Iakobson's typology. She equated Günsenin 1 (Ganos) amphorae with Iakobson's Type 4, which in turn could be correlated with fabric 4 (loose, tempered with grog, feldspar, quartzite, carbonates and pyroxene), fabric 5 (well-levigated, without sand), and fabric 6 (fine-grained sand and a fluidal structure). She regarded the amphorae of fabric 5 as Byzantine imports, while the others were locally produced wares.[198]

Iakobson described the pear-shaped amphorae with narrowly spaced grooving as the most distinctive tenth-century amphora type of Chersonesus, noting that they were often found together with coins of Romanos I, Constantine Porphyrogenitus, Romanos II and Basileus II. In his view, these had been produced locally.[199] These amphorae were also discussed at length by two Bulgarian scholars, Iordanka Changova and Liudmila Doncheva-Petkova. The latter assigned the pear-shaped amphorae with narrowly spaced ribbing to Variant A of Type 1 and dated them to the tenth century.[200]

Günsenin, after whom the amphora type was named, based her classification on the medieval amphorae housed in the collections of fifteen Turkish museums (among them Sinop and Samsun, two museums on the Black Sea), whose study she began in 1984. In her study published in 1989, she assigned the amphorae to four main types according to their form: Type 1 was represented by amphorae

---

[195] DEMANGEL – MAMBOURY 1939, 46, 148–149, Fig. 198.
[196] ЯКОБСОН 1951, 335–337.
[197] ПЛЕТНЕВА 1959, 244.
[198] ПЛЕТНЕВА 1963, 48–51, Рис. 32.
[199] ЯКОБСОН 1979, 70–73, Рис. 43/5–6.
[200] ДОНЧЕВА-ПЕТКОВА 1977, 98–101.

with a wide, short neck, short handles and ribbed, tapering body with a rounded base, fired to a brick red, orange or buff colour. Their height ranged between 28 and 48 cm, their width between 24 and 41 cm, and their rim diameter between 7 and 11.5 cm. Günsenin dated this type between the ninth and the eleventh centuries, and noted that they were widely distributed in the Sea of Marmara and Black Sea region.[201]

In her doctoral dissertation defended in 1990, Günsenin modified her initial classification and distinguished a few transitional types. She highlighted the extraordinary diversity of amphora types and noted that their form and dimension could vary considerably even within a single cargo. She assigned Type 1 amphorae to the early eleventh century, although she acknowledged that a date in the tenth century was also feasible, as in the case of the pieces found at Saraçhane. The type had a wide distribution and was attested in Constantinople, Antioch, Bulgaria, Romania and the northern Black Sea coast, and even as far as Otranto.[202] Günsenin described two transitional variants of Type 1; in her view, Types 3 and 4 developed from Type 1. She assigned the large, squat, globular amphorae to transitional types 1–4.[203]

The identification of the type's workshops remained one of the major tasks of subsequent research. In 1989, Günsenin began systematic field surveys in the area of the village of Şarköy near Tekirdağ, and discovered two dumps containing amphora wasters along the 5 km long coast between modern Hoşköy (antique Khora) and Gaziköy (antique Ganos). A magnetometer survey conducted in 1991 revealed traces of several pottery kilns and waster dumps.[204] During the excavation of the site in 1992 and 1993, Günsenin uncovered the kilns with a rectangular dome constructed from Type 1 amphora sherds, which she compared to the region's modern pottery kilns.[205]

Later, Günsenin continued her research on the islands of the Sea of Marmara (*Marmara adası*) and conducted underwater archaeological prospecting in 1993 and 1994, during which she identified eleven Byzantine shipwrecks, seven of which had a cargo of Ganos amphorae. The most important among these was the wreck found at the Tekmezar Burnu promontory.[206]

---

[201] GÜNSENIN 1989, 269–271.
[202] GÜNSENIN 1990, 21–24.
[203] GÜNSENIN 1990, 24–25, Fig. 12.
[204] GÜNSENIN 1993, 193–195.
[205] GÜNSENIN 1995, 165–175.
[206] GÜNSENIN 1998, 309–316; GÜNSENIN 1999, 18–23.

The most significant eleventh-century wreck with a cargo of Ganos amphorae was investigated at Serçe Limanı in southern Anatolia by the specialists of the Institute of Nautical Archaeology of Texas University between 1977 and 1979. The ship's main cargo was made up of glass vessels, but she had also carried fifty-six amphorae of this type. Known also as the glass wreck, the Serçe Limani shipwreck was dated to after 1025 on the testimony of the Fatimid glass weights.[207]

In addition to the investigations in the Sea of Marmara and the Aegean, research on this amphora type continued in the Don region and the Taman Peninsula too, leading to a more accurate and reliable typochronological sequence. In her re-assessment of the Sarkel occupation levels, Pletneva dated the type from the late ninth to the later eleventh centuries.[208] Chkhaidze described this type, occurring among the amphorae of Khazar-period Tmutarakan, as globular amphorae (*сфероемкостные*) and assigned them to the period between the later tenth and the early eleventh centuries. He underlined the high number of stamped amphorae within the type and described in detail an amphora with stamped handle found on the territory of the Taman fort.[209]

The study of Günsenin I amphorae was set in a wider context following a more detailed review of the Ganos wine trade. The amphorae were used for transporting wine made on the estates of the Ganos monastery and the current evidence suggests that in addition to the eastern Mediterranean, this wine was also traded to the Black Sea region and the Kievan Rus, and even as far as Lund and Sigtuna in Sweden. It enjoyed widespread popularity during the eleventh century in the Balkans after the restoration of Byzantine rule in the late tenth century – the finds from the Athenian agora indicate that the use of the amphora extended into the early twelfth century. The greatest market for sweet Ganos wine was undoubtedly Constantinople, as indicated by the two shipwrecks carrying Günsenin 1 amphorae uncovered in the Theodosian Port (*Portus Theodosiacus*, modern Yenikapı, Istanbul).[210]

Fabric and temper

The Günsenin 1 amphorae of the Sinop museum have a fine-grained micaceous fabric, occasionally with some fine-grained sand. This fine and uniform fabric

---

[207] Bass et al. 2004.
[208] Плетнева 2006, 219, Рис. 73/4.
[209] Чхаидзе 2008, 153–157.
[210] Günsenin 2009, 147–153.

reflects the use of finely levigated clay and the exploitation of the same clay deposits.

My observations on the fabric of the Sinop amphorae described and discussed here are consistent with the results of the earlier petrographic analyses and macroscopic observations. The amphorae from Tmutarakan were examined by Krug, whose findings were analysed by Pletneva, according to whom Type 4 (Ganos) amphorae were characterised by three fabrics: fabric 4 (loose, tempered with grog, feldspar, quartzite, carbonates and pyroxene), fabric 5 (well-levigated, without sand), and fabric 6 (fine-grained sand and a fluidal structure), of which she regarded vessels of fabric 5 as Byzantine imports, while the others were locally produced wares.[211] In this classification, the Sinop amphorae can be assigned to fabric 5. In 2003, V. V. Bulgakov and B. G. Iakovlev, specialists of the Ukrainian Academy of Sciences in Kiev, performed the petrographic analysis of seventeen Günsenin 1 amphorae and found that there was barely any difference between the fabric of ninth–tenth-century and twelfth–thirteenth-century Byzantine amphorae, suggesting that they had been produced in the same workshops.[212] Judging from the similar mineral contents of the amphora fragments found there, the workshop can probably be identified with the amphora kilns discovered by Günsenin on the coast between modern Hoşköy (antique Khora) near Tekirdağ and Gaziköy (antique Ganos) during her field surveys and magnetometer survey,[213] which she excavated in 1992–1993.[214]

Ganos amphorae were carefully fired to an even colour; the vessels have a clear ringing tone when tapped, but their fabric is often soft and crumbly. Most of the amphorae assigned to this type are orange, but pieces with a pinkish hue also occur. The most frequent colours according to the Munsell Colour Chart are shades of pink (5 YR 7/4: Nos 33–34, 37, 46; 7.5 YR: Nos 42, 44), followed by shades of reddish-yellow (5 YR 7/6: Nos 38, 41, 45; 7.5 YR 6/6: Nos 47, 49). The other hues (5 YR 5/4, 5 YR 5/6, 5 YR 6/4, 5 YR 6/6, 7.5 YR 7/6) were typical for a single amphora each.

In sum, the amphorae can be regarded as rather uniform in terms of their petrography and the quality of their firing, suggesting that they had been produced in the same workshop.

---

[211] Плетнева 1963, 48–51, Рис. 32.

[212] Булгаков – Яковлев 2003.

[213] Günsenin 1993, 193–195.

[214] Günsenin 1995, 165–175.

Formal classification and metric data

The amphorae assigned to this type all have a straight, slightly thickened rim with a stepped interior. The rim in narrow: the exterior rim diameter ranges between 8.3 and 12.2 cm, the interior one between 5 and 8.2 cm. The neck of Günsenin 1 amphorae is slender (6.6–9.4 cm) and short (1–7.8 cm), the vessels have a pear-shaped, tapering body with the greatest diameter at the shoulder and a rounded base.

No formal variants can be distinguished among the amphorae with more or less identical form and proportions, even though some pieces differ slightly owing to their short neck. At the same time, two variants can be noted regarding size: most Günsenin 1 amphorae are small and have a short, cylindrical neck, but there is also a larger variant without a neck, on which the rim blends directly into the shoulder. These two groups formed separate clusters in both cluster analyses of the Ganos amphorae from Sinop. Both analyses were based on three size attributes: the first on height, greatest diameter and exterior rim diameter, the second on height, greatest diameter and neck height.

The smaller amphorae (Group a) have a height ranging between 35 and 42 cm and a greatest diameter ranging from 27 to 33.1 cm. The neck can be as tall as 7.8 cm. The larger amphorae generally stand between 43 and 47.5 cm tall and their greatest diameter exceeds by far that of the other group (35.6–41.7 cm), while the maximum height of their neck is a mere 2 cm. Günsenin had already pointed out these differences in the dimensions of the amphorae and she also noted that different sizes of the same type (Type 1) occur in ship cargos (Serçe Limanı, Hayırsız Ada, Kötü Burun).[215] Frederick van Doorninck identified some two dozen size ranges among the Ganos amphorae in the cargo of the eleventh-century Serçe Limanı shipwreck, a forceful counter-argument to suggestions of the existence of a standardised metrology in the period resembling the one that characterised late antiquity.[216]

There is but a single type among the medieval amphorae from Sinop that differs regarding its form, which can be seen as an early variant of Günsenin 1 amphorae. Three exemplars can be assigned to this variant (Nos 33–35), which can be described as having an everted, thickened and rounded rim and an angular handle with a double groove down its length springing from under the rim to the shoulder.

[215] GÜNSENIN 1990, 22.

[216] VAN DOORNINCK 1993, 8–12; VAN DOORNINCK 2002, 904–905.

Ornamentation, stamps and graffiti

The entire body of Günsenin 1 amphorae is covered with dense ribbing with wide, shallow grooves in-between that terminate in a spiral on the rounded base. Although the amphorae representing this type are often covered with a white slip, no traces of a coating could be noted on the Sinop amphorae, perhaps because all were found in the sea and their surface was damaged. Ribbing and slipping cannot be regarded as ornamentation in the strict sense, but rather as a surface treatment. Some amphorae have a stamped handle and graffiti incised on the shoulder after firing. Their meaning is still debated: they have been variously interpreted as indicating the amphora's contents or capacity, an owner's mark or even an imperial mark.

Stamps are rare on the Günsenin 1 amphorae from Sinop. One amphora of the early variant with angular handles bears a rectangular stamp with a Greek monogram (of which the letters *Π* and *A* are legible) on the upper part of one handle near the rim. Parshina contended that amphora production was an imperial monopoly and that the stamps represented the Byzantine emperors' monograms between 843 and 1143. Although this interpretation can be challenged, one of her remarks, namely that the stamps appearing on the handles were generally rectangular in the ninth–tenth centuries and that they were replaced by round ones from the late tenth or early eleventh century onwards, remains highly relevant.[217]

A round stamp occurs on a single amphora from Sinop (No. 44): a circular cogwheel-like stamp impressed before firing under the neck, near one of the handles. Similar stamps have been published from Istanbul, Edirne, Serçe Limanı and Dinogetia.[218]

Several amphorae assigned to this type are inscribed. Most of the inscriptions are made up of letters scratched onto the vessels with a sharp tool after firing, but in one case (No. 37), the letters *I* and *ω* (perhaps an abbreviation of the name Ioannés) were incised before firing. The *I ω* ligature is relatively common in the round stamps on Ganos amphorae, for example on pieces from Constantinople, Athens, Dinogetia and Sarkel,[219] as well as from Kirazlıköy near Ganos itself. In Günsenin's interpretation, the monogram was the mark of an amphora potter called Ioannés.[220]

---

[217] Паршина 2001, 109–115; see also Grünbart – Lochner-Metaxas 2002, 186–188.
[218] Günsenin 1990, Fig. 43.
[219] Günsenin 1990, I. Fig. 43.
[220] Günsenin 1993, 201, Figs 9–10.

Letters incised after firing are more frequent, occurring on four Sinop amphorae. The letters *K* and *E* occur on the shoulder of one amphora (No. 46), an inverted letter *M* whose stems were underlined by the handle on another one (No. 34), a third bears a large *Λ* and *N* immediately beside the handle (No. 48), while the graffito under the handle on a fourth amphora is illegible (No. 38). Comparable graffiti are known from the Crimea: *K*+*E* ligatures occur on the amphorae found by the harbour of Chersonesus.[221]

Origins and distribution

Günsenin 1 amphorae were produced in the workshops along the 4 km long coastal section between Hoşköy (antique Khora) near Tekirdağ and Gaziköy (antique Ganos). The amphora kilns were identified after the discovery of waster dumps, first through field surveys and magnetometer surveys,[222] followed by Günsenin's excavation of the kilns in 1992–1993.[223] The Ganos origin of the amphorae from the Serçe Limani shipwreck was confirmed by the chemical analyses performed by Helen Hatcher.[224] Thus, the production site of the amphora type could be conclusively determined. Günsenin associated the production of the amphorae with the Ganos monastic communities and the wineries maintained by them.[225]

The location of the workshop area on the Sea of Marmara and its proximity to Constantinople (*ca.* 200 km) suggest a large-scale centralisation and the contraction of trade networks, despite the type's extensive distribution. In 1990, Günsenin wrote of a distribution extending from Antioch to Sarkel and Otranto in Italy;[226] ten years later, this distribution was extended to Egypt and Sweden (Lund, Sigtuna) on the testimony of new finds.[227]

Chronology

According to the type's generally accepted chronology, Ganos amphorae can be dated between the later ninth and the close of the eleventh centuries, although there is some disagreement between scholars regarding finer details and a typological

[221] Романчук 1983, Рис. 2, 7п.
[222] Günsenin 1993, 193–195.
[223] Günsenin 1995, 165–175.
[224] Günsenin – Hatcher 1997, 249–260.
[225] Günsenin 1993, 195–196; Günsenin 2009, 150–152.
[226] Günsenin 1990, 23–24.
[227] Günsenin 2009, 153, Fig. 10.2.

development can also be noted. The amphorae of this type brought to light at Chersonesus were dated to the ninth–eleventh centuries by coins of Basileus I (867–886) and Basileus II (976–1025).[228] At Sarkel, this type was recovered from the settlement's Rus occupation levels (late tenth–eleventh centuries),[229] while in Chersonesus, Ganos amphorae were found in association with the coins of Romanos I Lekapenos (920–944), Constantine Porphyrogenitus (913–959), Romanos II (953–959) and Basileus II (976–1025).[230]

The above chronology is also confirmed by the shipwreck finds: the so-called glass wreck found off the southern Anatolian coast at Serçe Limanı is dated to after 1025 by the Fatimid glass weights.[231] Chkhaidze assigned the amphorae found in the occupation levels of Tmutarakan between the later tenth and the early eleventh centuries,[232] while the finds from the Athenian agora indicated that Ganos amphorae remained in use until the early twelfth century.[233]

Function

In view of their production centre and the associated evidence, Günsenin 1 amphorae were used for transporting the sweet wine made on the estates of the Ganos monastery, far famed in the tenth–eleventh centuries.[234] Unfortunately, the graffiti scratched onto the vessels after firing reveal nothing about their contents. Nevertheless, their use as wine amphorae seems likely because the Tekirdağ area is still one of the major wine producing areas in Turkey.

Catalogue

(a) Tall-necked Günsenin 1 amphorae (late ninth–early tenth century)

33. Amphora *(Plate 33)*
Inv. no. 3.3.12
Find context: purchase from Şükrü Özdemir, resident of Ayancık (March 6, 2012)
Pink (5 YR 7/4), well-fired amphora tempered with fine-grained sand and mica; hard fabric. Everted, thickened, folded rim with cylindrical exterior and curved interior,

---

228 Якобсон 1951, 335–337.
229 Плетнева 1959, 244.
230 Якобсон 1979, 70–73.
231 Bass et al. 2004.
232 Чхаидзе 2008, 153–157.
233 Günsenin 2009, 147–149.
234 Günsenin 1990, I. 57–61; Günsenin 2009, 151–152.

with the wheel turning marks clearly visible and tangible in the interior; relatively tall, cylindrical neck; pear-shaped body with the greatest diameter in the upper third and a transition between the body and the rounded base. The angular, oval-sectioned handles spring from immediately underneath the rim to the shoulder. One handle has a rectangular stamp with the letters *Π* and *A*. The body is covered with narrowly spaced ribbing from the neck downward, continuing in spiral groove on the vessel base. The stamped handle is grooved.
H. 42 cm, diam. 32.25 cm, rim diam. 12.2 cm (ext.), 8.2 cm (int.), rim H. 2 cm, rim Th. 2.3 cm, rim fold 1.5 cm, neck diam. 9.4 cm, neck H. 6.9 cm, left handle H. 12 cm (ext.), 7 cm (int.), left handle W. 4.1 cm, left handle Th. 2.7 cm, right handle H. 12 cm (ext.), 7.1 cm (int.), right handle W. 4.2 cm, right handle Th. 2.5 cm, rib W. 0.5 cm, stamp 2 cm x 1.5 cm

34. Amphora *(Plate 34)*
Inv. no. 3.6.90
Reg. no. 2948
Find context: from the Black Sea, purchase from fisherman Şükrü Gümüş, resident of Sinop (Yenimahalle, Vali sokak) (June 14, 1990)
Date: later ninth–earlier tenth century
Pink (5 YR 7/4) amphora tempered with fine-grained sand and mica; hard fabric, clear ringing tone when tapped. Everted rim with folded, straight, cylindrical exterior and curved interior; relatively tall, conical neck; pear-shaped body with the greatest diameter in the upper third and a transition between the body and the rounded base. The angular, oval-sectioned handle with multiple grooves down the centre springs from under the rim to the shoulder (one handle is lacking). The body is covered with ribbing from the neck downward, continuing in a spiral groove on the base. A graffiti of an underlined inverted M shape incised after firing can be seen above the inventory number near the missing handle and two small incised lines forming an X and a vertical line beside them on the opposite side near the other handle.
H. 41.8 cm, diam. 31.83 cm, rim diam. 11.3 cm (ext.), 7.4 cm (int.), rim H. 1.7 cm, rim Th. 1.8 cm, neck diam. 7.8 cm, neck H. 7.8 cm, handle H. 12.2 cm (ext.), 7.7 cm (ext.), handle W. 4.3 cm, handle Th. 2.5 cm, rib W. 0.7 cm, graffiti H 3.2 cm, X sign 1.8 cm, M sign 1.8 cm

35. Amphora *(Plate 35)*
Inv. no. 4.4.82
Reg. no. 2394
Find context: from the Black Sea, purchase from Ali Arslan, resident of Kuşlucaköy, Trabzon (November 24, 1982)
Date: later ninth–earlier tenth century

Reddish-brown amphora (5 YR 5/4) tempered with fine-grained sand and mica; hard fabric, clear ringing tone when tapped. Everted, rounded, folded rim; relatively tall, conical neck; pear-shaped body with the greatest diameter in the upper third, conical lower part and angular transition between the body and the rounded base. The flat, oval-sectioned, angular handles spring from the immediately under the rim to the shoulder. The body is covered with relatively narrowly spaced ribbing with wide, shallow grooves in-between from the neck to the base, which is smooth.
H. 37 cm, diam. 26.89 cm, rim diam. 8.4 cm (ext.), 5 cm (int.), rim H. 1 cm, rim Th. 1 cm, neck diam. 7.5 cm, neck H. 5.2 cm, left handle H. (ext.) 9.2 cm, 4.9 cm (int.), left handle W. 3 cm, left handle Th. 2.3 cm, right handle H. 9.6 cm (ext.), 5.5 cm (int.), right handle W. 3.4 cm, right handle Th. 2 cm, rib W. 0.8 cm, groove W. 0.5 cm

(b) Small variants

36. Amphora *(Plate 36)*
Inv. no. 1.3.85
Reg. no. 2829
Find context: from the Black Sea, purchase from Erdal Batmaz, resident of Sinop (Batmazlar Motoru) (December 19, 1985)
Light reddish-brown (5 YR 6/4) amphora tempered with fine-grained mica; soft fabric, clear ringing tone when tapped. Slightly everted, thickened rim with straight exterior and curved interior; short, straight neck; pear-shaped body with the greatest diameter in the upper third, tapering in the lower third; rounded base. The short, squat, arched, oval-sectioned handles rising slightly above the rim spring from under the rim (in part from the rim) to the shoulder. The vessel body is ribbed from the neck downward, ending in a spiral groove on the base. Iron-oxide residue can be noted on a section above the shoulder.
H. 38 cm, diam. 33.1 cm, rim diam. 9 cm (ext.), 6.4 cm (int.), rim H. 2 cm, rim Th. 1 cm, neck diam. 7 cm, neck H. 3 cm, left handle H. 11.8 cm (ext.), 6.6 cm (int.), left handle W. 3.9 cm, left handle Th. 2.3 cm, right handle H. 10.8 cm (ext.), 6.5 cm (int.), right handle W. 3.8, right handle Th. 2.4 cm, rib W. 0.5 cm

37. Amphora *(Plate 37)*
Inv. no. 1.13.89
Reg. no. 2912
Find context: purchase from fisherman Şükrü Gümüş, resident of Sinop (August 18, 1989)
Pink (5 YR 7/4), well-fired amphora tempered with fine-grained sand and mica; soft fabric, clear ringing tone when tapped. Short, straight, slightly thickened folded rim; short, cylindrical, stepped, ribbed neck; oval body with the greatest diameter in the upper third, transition between the body and the rounded base. The short, squat, slightly arched, oval-sectioned handles spring from the ribbed neck under the rim to the shoulder, but do

not rise above the rim. The body is covered with ribbing from the neck downward to the base, ending in a spiral groove on the base. The letters *I* and *ω* (?Ioannés) incised before firing can be seen between the two handles under the neck.
H. 39.5 cm, diam. 32.14 cm, rim diam. 9.1 cm (ext.), 6.5 cm (int.), rim H. 1.5 cm, neck diam. 7.2 cm, neck H. 3.3 cm, left handle H. 12.2 cm (ext.), 6.9 cm (int.), left handle W. 4.1 cm, left handle Th. 2.3 cm, right handle H. 12.3 cm (ext.), 7.2 cm (ext.), right handle W. 4.3 cm, right handle Th. 2.5 cm, rib W. 0.5 cm, inscription 1.5 cm x 2.6 cm

38. Amphora *(Plate 38)*
Inv. no. 10.1.07
Reg. no. 3495
Find context: from the Black Sea, donated by the Coast Guard, Sinop (2007)
Date: later tenth–early eleventh century
Reddish-yellow (5 YR 7/6), well-fired amphora tempered with fine-grained mica. Short, straight, folded rim with smooth interior; short, tapering neck; pear-shaped body with a transition between the body and the base. The slightly arched, oval-sectioned handles, each with a light groove down the centre, spring from under the rim to the shoulder. The greater part of the vessel body is ribbed from the lower handle attachment to the body-base transition, underneath which the groove of the ribbing continues in a wide spiral. There is a graffiti incised with a sharp tool under the left handle.
H. 36 cm, diam. 28.17 cm, rim diam. 8.4 cm (ext.), 5.8 cm (int.), rim H. 2.4 cm, rim Th. 1.6 cm, neck diam. 6.6 cm, neck H. 2.2 cm, left handle H. 12 cm (ext.), 6.7 cm (int.), left handle W. 3.8 cm, left handle Th. 2.4 cm, right handle H. 11.5 cm (ext.), 5.2 cm (int.), right handle W. 3.7 cm, right handle Th. 2.5 cm, rib W. 0.6 cm, graffiti L. 1.7 cm

39. Amphora *(Plate 39)*
Inv. no. 10.8.1981
Reg. no. 2358
Find context: purchase from Mustafa Arslan, resident of Sinop (December 8, 1981)
Date: later ninth–early tenth century
Reddish-yellow (5 YR 6/6) well-fired amphora; hard fabric, clear ringing tone when tapped. Everted, rounded rim; short, conical neck; pear-shaped body with the greatest diameter in the upper third, a transition at the shoulder and the base, and a rounded base. The wide, relatively flat, slightly arched, oval-sectioned handles spring from just below the rim to above the shoulder. The body is ribbed with deep, relatively narrow grooves in-between from the neck downward, more narrowly spaced above the shoulder than underneath it, where it becomes more widely spaced; the ribbing extends to the body-base transition, but not to the smooth base.
H. 35.5 cm, diam. 29.9 cm, rim diam. 8 cm x 9 cm (ext.), 5.9 cm (int.), rim H. 1.2 cm, rim Th. 1 cm, neck diam. 8 cm, neck H. 5 cm, left handle H. 9.2 cm (ext.), 5.5 cm (int.), left

handle W. 3.7 cm, left handle Th. 2 cm, right handle H. 9.5 cm (ext.), 6.3 cm (ext.), right handle W. 3.2 cm, right handle Th. 2 cm, rib W. 1 cm

40. Amphora *(Plate 40)*
Inv. no. 10.13.81
Reg. no. 2363
Find context: purchase from Mustafa Arslan, resident of Sinop (December 8, 1981)
Date: later tenth–earlier eleventh century
Reddish-yellow (5 YR 7/6), well-fired amphora tempered with fine-grained mica, covered with a white slip; clear ringing tone when tapped. Slightly everted, thickened rim, broken in some spots; short, cylindrical neck; oval body, strongly tapering towards the base, with a transition between the body and the gently rounded base. The curved, oval-sectioned handles with convex exterior and flat underside spring from below the rim to the shoulder. One handle has a shallow groove down the centre. The body is covered with ribbing from the neck downward, ending in a spiral groove on the vessel base. There is a gap in the ribbing at the body-base transition. A profusion of incised signs can be seen in line with the shoulders (see the detail photo).
H. 37 cm, diam. 29.76 cm, rim diam. 8.8 cm (ext.), 6.6 cm (int.), rim H. 1.85 cm, rim Th. 1.1 cm, neck diam. 6.8 cm, neck H. 3.5 cm, left handle H. 11.7 cm (ext.), 6.7 cm (int.), left handle W. 3.6 cm, left handle Th. 2.5 cm, right handle H. 11.8 cm (ext.), 6.3 cm (ext.), right handle W. 3.5 cm, right handle Th. 2.3 cm, rib W. 0.4 cm

41. Amphora *(Plate 41)*
Inv. no. 11.3.83
Reg. no. 2596
Find context: purchase from fisherman Tayfun Güner, resident of Sinop (July 6, 1983)
Date: later tenth century
Reddish-yellow (5 YR 7/6), well-fired amphora; soft fabric, dull tone when tapped. Short, slightly thickened folded rim with smooth interior; short, cylindrical neck; wide pear-shaped body with the greatest diameter in the upper third and a transition between the body and the rounded base. The, curved, wide, oval-sectioned handles spring from directly under the rim to the shoulder. The body is covered with ribbing from the lower handle attachment downward to the body-base transition, not extending to the smooth base. The ribbing is more narrowly spaced on the shoulder than on the lower part of the vessel body. There are no graffiti on the amphora.
H. 38 cm, diam. 29.28 cm, rim diam. 8.8 cm (ext.), 7.2 cm (int.), rim H. 2 cm, rim Th. 1 cm, neck diam. 7 cm, neck H. 3.5 cm, left handle H. 11 cm (ext.), 6.3 cm (int.), left handle W. 3.6 cm, left handle Th. 2.6 cm, right handle H. 13.2 cm (ext.), 8.2 cm (int.), right handle W. 4 cm, right handle Th. 3 cm

42. Amphora *(Plate 42)*
Inv. no. 14.5.82
Reg. no. 2420
Find context: donated by fisherman Rifat Reis, resident of Sinop (December 30, 1982)
Date: later tenth–earlier eleventh century
Pink (7.5 YR 7/4), well-fired amphora tempered with fine-grained mica; soft fabric. Slightly everted, thickened rim with a shallow circumferential groove underneath; upward widening, short, straight, conical neck; pear-shaped body tapering towards the base, with prominent transitions at the shoulder and above the rounded base. The vessel body is squattish. The arched, oval-sectioned handle rising slightly above the rim springs from under the rim to the shoulder (one handle broke off). The body is covered with ribbing from the neck downward to the base, which is smooth. A sign incised after firing can be seen under the lower handle attachment point of the missing handle: an X sign enclosed within a square set on its tip. One side of the amphora between the handles has long straight lines incised after firing: two vertical lines with two horizontal lines on top and a *Λ*-like sign beside them.
H. 36.5 cm, diam. 30.87 cm, rim diam. 8.7 cm (ext.), 6.6 cm (int.), rim H. 1.25 cm, rim Th. 1 cm, neck diam. 7 cm, neck H. 3.1 cm, handle H. 12.6 cm 9 (ext.), 7.1 cm (int.), handle W. 3.5 cm, handle Th. 2.5 cm, rib W. 0.75 cm, rib Th. 1.2 cm, sign L. 9.5–10 cm

43. Amphora *(Plate 43)*
Inv. no. 15.1.89
Find context: from the Black Sea, from the area of the inner harbour at Sinop (İç Liman), purchase from İzzet Aşir
Date: late ninth–earlier tenth century
Yellowish-red (5 YR 5/6), well-fired amphora tempered with fine-grained sand and some mica; hard fabric, clear ringing tone when tapped. Rounded folded rim; short conical neck; pear-shaped body tapering to a conical lower part with a transition between the body and the rounded base. The angular, flat, oval-sectioned handles lack any ribbing or grooving and spring directly from under the rim to the shoulder. The body is ribbed from the lower handle attachment downward to beyond the body-base transition, but the base itself is smooth. There is a large oval hole in the base and two smaller ones on the body. The rim, the neck and the handles are covered with shells and marine sediment.
H. 35.5 cm, diam. 27.53 cm, rim diam. 8.3 cm (ext.), 5.4 cm (int.), rim H. 1.4 cm, rim Th. 1.4 cm, neck diam. 7 cm, neck H. 4.8 cm, left handle H. 10.6 cm (ext.), 5.5 cm (int.), left handle W. 3.6 cm, left handle Th. 2.4 cm, right handle H. 10.4 cm (ext.), 5.7 cm (int.), right handle W. 3.6 cm, right handle Th. 2.3 cm, rib W. 0.8 cm

44. Amphora *(Plate 44)*
Inv. no. 20.8.82
Reg. no. 2461

Find context: from the museum's old collection, originally housed in the Pervane madrasah (June 24, 1983)
Date: late tenth–earlier eleventh century
Pink (7.5 YR 7/4), well-fired amphora tempered with fine-grained mica; soft fabric, clear ringing tone when tapped. Slightly everted, thickened rim with a groove around the rim interior; extremely short, straight neck; pear-shaped body with the greatest diameter in the upper third and a transition between the body and the rounded base. The arched handle rising slightly above the rim springs from under the rim to above the shoulder (one handle broke off). The body is covered with narrowly spaced ribbing beginning under the rim and extending to the base where it is slightly worn and cannot be clearly made out. The ribbing ends in a spiral groove on the base. There is a round impressed motif with deep sharp contours resembling a cogwheel underneath the surviving handle.
H. 39 cm, diam. 30.71 cm, rim diam. 9 cm (ext.), 6.2 cm (int.), rim H. 2.6 cm, rim Th. 1.2 cm, neck diam. 7.2 cm, neck H. 1 cm, handle H. 11 cm (ext.), 6.2 cm (int.), handle W. 3.8 cm, handle Th. 2.6 cm, rib W. 0.6 cm, stamp diam. 2 cm (ext.), 1.5 cm (int.)

45. Amphora *(Plate 45)*
Inv. no. 36.5.80
Reg. no. 2314
Find context: purchase from fisherman Mustafa Arslan, resident of Sinop (Tersane) (January 22, 1981)
Date: later tenth–earlier eleventh century
Reddish-yellow (5 YR 7/6) amphora tempered with fine-grained mica, covered with a translucent white slip; clear ringing tone when tapped. Short, straight, slightly thickened rim with smooth interior, tapering towards the neck; short, straight neck, narrower under the rim, covered with the upper handle attachments for the greater part; oval body with the greatest diameter in the upper third, conical lower half and rounded base, with a transition between the body and the base. The short, arched, oval-sectioned handles spring from the neck under the rim; the left handle bears a *Λ*-like incision, the right one a shallow groove down its centre. The lower handle attachments are above the shoulder. The body is covered with ribbing from the neck downward to the base, becoming somewhat wider and more widely spaced towards the base. A sign made up of an X-shaped mark and a vertical line was incised after firing above the shoulder between the two handles.
H. 35 cm, diam. 32.46 cm, rim diam. 9.1 cm (ext.), 7 cm (int.), rim H. 2 cm, rim Th. 1.3 cm, neck diam. 6.8 cm, neck H. 3.2 cm, left handle H. 10.3 cm (ext.), 6.2 cm (int.), left handle W. 3.75 cm, left handle Th. 2.5 cm, right handle H. 11.7 cm (ext.), 6 cm (int.), right handle W. 4 cm, right handle Th. 2.6 cm, incised sign L. 7.3 cm, incised sign W. 4.5 cm

(c) Large variant

46. Amphora *(Plate 46)*
Inv. no. 1.11.89
Reg. no. 2910
Find context: purchase from fisherman Şükrü Gümüş, resident of Sinop (August 18, 1989)
Pink (5 YR 7/4), well-fired amphora tempered with fine-grained mica and sand; soft fabric, dull tone when tapped. Short, straight, cylindrical rim with a deep circumferential groove under the rim and a groove around the rim interior; pear-shaped body with the greatest diameter in the upper third and the lower third tapering towards the rounded base. The thick, arched, oval-sectioned handles spring from under the rim (in part from the rim) and rise above the rim before attaching to the area above the shoulder. The body is ribbed from the rim downward, more narrowly spaced on the upper part with deep, wide grooves around the shoulder and the grooves spiralling down to the base. There is a graffiti incised with a sharp tool on the shoulder (beside the inventory number), of which a *K* and an *E* can be made out.
H. 44.5 cm, diam. 35.65 cm, rim diam. 8.8 cm (ext.), 6.73 cm (int.), rim H. 2.02 cm, rim Th. 1.5 cm, left handle H. 13.3 cm (ext.), 6.5 cm (int.), left handle W. 3.7 cm, left handle Th. 2.5 cm, right handle H. 12.5 cm (ext.), 6.6 cm (int.), right handle W. 4 cm, right handle Th. 2.7 cm, rib W. 0.5 cm, graffiti L. 5.3 cm (letter *K*)

47. Amphora *(Plate 47)*
Inv. no. 3.20.73
Find context: from the Black Sea, purchase from fisherman Şükrü Gümüş, resident of Sinop (Tersane caddesi) (1973)
Date: later eleventh century
Reddish-yellow (7.5 YR 6/6), well-fired amphora tempered with very fine-grained mica; clear ringing tone when tapped. Straight, short, thickened, folded rim; short, straight neck, narrower than the vessel body; pear-shaped body with the greatest diameter in the upper third, continuing in a conical form from the shoulder, with a transition between the body and the rounded base. The short, curved, thick, oval-sectioned handles spring from the upper edge of the rim to above the shoulder; there is a groove at the upper attachment end of the left handle. The body's upper third is covered with ribbing extending to below the shoulder, the remainder of the body is covered with more widely spaced, wider ribs, the grooving in-between the ribs continues on the vessel base and ends in a spiral. There are closely spaced, deeply incised lines below the neck above the shoulder: two *Λ* signs with two triangles and straight lines underneath.
H. 44.5 cm, diam. 40.42 cm, rim diam. 8.5 cm (ext.), 5.6 cm (int.), rim H. 2.1 cm, rim Th. 1.6 cm, neck diam. 8 cm, neck H. 1.4 cm, left handle H. 14.3 cm (ext.), 8.2 cm (int.), left handle W. 4.1 cm, left handle Th. 2.8 cm, right handle H. 12.2 cm (ext.), 6.8 cm (int.),

right handle W. 3.8 cm, right handle Th. 2.5 cm, rib W. 0.5 cm, graffito L. 6.4 cm, graffito W. 8.6 cm

48. Amphora *(Plate 48)*
Inv. no. 7.1.97
Find context: purchase from Aysun Gezginci, resident of Sinop (1997)
Date: later eleventh century
Reddish-yellow (5 YR 7/8), well-fired amphora tempered with fine-grained mica; soft fabric, clear ringing tone when tapped. Short, thickened, folded rim with a circumferential groove underneath and one around the rim interior; no neck; pear-shaped body with the greatest diameter in the upper third, conical lower part and a transition between the body and the rounded base. The thick, slightly arched, oval-sectioned handles, each with a barely prominent rib down the centre, spring from the rim and rise above the rim before attaching to above the shoulder. The greater part of the body is covered with ribbing, more narrowly spaced with deep grooves in-between on the shoulder and with shallower grooves on the lower third. The ribbing extends to the base, continuing in a spiral groove on the base. There are graffiti incised after firing under the handle and on the front side: a large *Λ* and an inverted *N* with a + sign above it under one handle and a longer graffiti of a large *Λ*, a smaller *Λ* and a *H* under the other.
H. 47.5 cm, diam. 41.22 cm, rim diam. 9.1 cm (ext.), 6.7 cm (int.), rim H. 1.7 cm, rim Th. 1.3 cm, left handle H. 14 cm (ext.), 7 cm (int.), left handle W. 3.9 cm, left handle Th. 3.1 cm, right handle H. 12.8 cm (ext.), 6.5 cm (int.), right handle W. 3.7 cm, right handle Th. 2.7 cm, rib W. 0.45 cm, graffiti L. 9.9 cm, lower groove depth 0.6 cm

49. Amphora *(Plate 49)*
Inv. no. 21.4.82
Reg. no. 2489
Find context: purchase from Sayin Arslan, resident of Istanbul, Sarıyer (September 7, 1983)
Date: eleventh century
Reddish-yellow (7.5 YR 6/6), well-fired amphora tempered with very fine-grained mica; soft fabric, clear ringing tone when tapped. Short, thickened, folded rim with an undercut; there is no neck; the rounded, pear-shaped body begins immediately under the rim and tapers towards the base with a slight transition at the greatest diameter. The arched, oval-sectioned handles spring from the rim, one rising slightly above the rim before attaching to above the shoulder, the other is less arched. The lower handle attachments were carefully smoothed. The fabric is very soft and the ribbing is worn in several spots. The body is ribbed from the rim downward to the shoulder, there is a band of deep ribbing under the shoulder followed by an "empty" band where the ribbing is worn; the ribbing continues to the rounded base, which is plain.

H. 43 cm, diam. 36.92 cm, rim diam. 9 cm (ext.), 6.6 cm (int.), rim H. 2.3 cm, rim Th. 1.3 cm, neck diam. 7 cm, neck H. 2 cm, handle H. 13 cm (ext.), 8.4 cm (int.), handle W. 3.7 cm handle Th. 3.2 cm, rib W. 0.7 cm, rib Th. 0.8 cm

50. Amphora *(Plate 50)*
Inv. no. 22.1.77
Find context: from the Black Sea, purchase from Necati Çor, resident of Sinop (İncedayı mahallesi) (1977)
Date: later eleventh century
Reddish-yellow (7.5 YR 7/6), well-fired amphora tempered with very fine-grained sand and mica; clear ringing tone when tapped. Short, slightly thickened, folded rim with a groove around the rim interior; no neck; pear-shaped body with the greatest diameter in the upper third, tapering towards the rounded base. The squat, arched, triangular-sectioned handle springs from the rim and rises above the rim before attaching to the shoulder above the greatest diameter (one handle broke off). The body is ribbed from the rim downward to the upper two-thirds, followed by an almost plain band with barely prominent ribbing and with more prominent ribbing underneath down to the vessel base.
H. 46 cm, diam. 41.69 cm, rim diam. 8.9 cm (ext.), 6.6 cm (int.), rim H. 1.8 cm, rim Th. 1 cm, neck diam. 8.5 cm, handle H. 14 cm (ext.), 8 cm (int.), handle W. 3.9 cm, handle Th. 2.9 cm, rib W. 0.6 cm (shoulder), 0.8 cm (belly), 0.7 cm (base), empty band W. 7.3 cm

Tmutarakan jugs

The collection of the Sinop Archaeological Museum includes thirteen tall, slender, long-necked jugs. These vessels were made from carefully levigated clay tempered with sand or pyroxene and fired to an orange-reddish colour. All have a short, straight rim with a circumferential groove, a tall cylindrical or slightly funnel-shaped neck, a wide, flat strap handle, an oval body and a flat base. Some have a linear decoration around the neck or shoulder incised before firing, other jugs are ornamented with a grooved pattern or two rows of punctates on the handle.

Research history

Tmutarakan jugs are also known as tall-necked, flat-handled jugs (*высокогорлые кувшини с плоскими ручками*, abbreviated as *ВКПР*)[235] in the Russian archaeological literature. Following A. A. Miller's excavations on the Taman Peninsula in 1930–31, the type was first distinguished and described by I. I.

[235] Чхаидзе 2008, 161.

Liapushkin, who noted the black pitch- or resin-like residue covering the jugs' interior, which according to the analyses performed in the laboratory of the Institute of the History of Material Culture of the Academy of Sciences of the Soviet Union in Leningrad was identified as pine resin.[236] Tmutarakan jugs were discussed in several comprehensive studies covering the transport and storage vessels of the northern Black Sea coast (Crimean and Taman Peninsulas) and the Don region, and there have been several proposals for their classification and chronological assignation.[237] Various chemical analyses have also contributed to studies on this vessel type.[238]

Iakobson can be credited with the first comprehensive treatment of this vessel type: in addition to providing a detailed formal and technical description, he also determined their chronological position in the ninth–tenth centuries based on the occupation levels dated by Chersonesus coins, noting that some of the vessels had been produced in Sarkel.[239] Until quite recently, Pletneva's studies on the pottery finds from Sarkel[240] and Tmutarakan,[241] covering also temper types and the vessel's sub-types based on body proportions, were the most comprehensive and most oft-quoted reference works in this field of research. In addition to the Black Sea jugs often covered with pitch in their interior, Pletneva distinguished locally made pieces tempered with large quantities of sand that had been unevenly fired in the ceramic inventory from Sarkel,[242] which she dated to between the eighth and eleventh centuries and believed to have originated from the Taman Peninsula owing to their abundance at Tmutarakan.[243]

Tmutarakan jugs have been found on all the ninth–tenth-century sites of the Crimean and Taman Peninsulas, and thus they appear in all the amphora and pottery analyses discussing the region's ceramics. I. A. Antonova and her colleagues described these vessels as flat-handled amphora-jugs (*кувшины-амфоры*) in their assessment of the medieval amphorae from Chersonesus, and

---

[236] Ляпушкин 1941, 207.

[237] Якобсон 1951, 337–338, Рис. 10/29–32; Якобсон 1979, Рис. 14, 1–4, 43, 8–10; Плетнева 1959, 248–251; Плетнева 1963, 52–59; Антонова et al. 1971, 91–92, Рис. 20–21; Романчук – Сазанов – Седикова 1995, 63–65, Табл. 30–32; Sazanov 1997, 97, Fig. 4/44; Чхаидзе 2008, 161–173.

[238] Ляпушкин 1941, 207; Кострин 1967, 285–289.

[239] Якобсон 1951, 337–338, Рис. 10/29–32; Якобсон 1979, Рис. 14, 1–4, 43, 8–10.

[240] Плетнева 1959, 248–251.

[241] Плетнева 1963, 52–59.

[242] Плетнева 1959, 249.

[243] Плетнева 1963, 54.

distinguished several variants based on the dimensions and wall thickness of the jugs.[244] The jugs played a prominent role in the study of the Byzantine amphorae from Chersonesus: Alla I. Romanchuk, Andrei V. Sazanov and Larisa V. Sedikova distinguished three main types based on the vessel form.[245]

The by far the most detailed study of these jugs can be found in Chkhaidze's monograph on Khazar-period Tmutarakan (Tamatarkha), in which he devoted a lengthy section to the discussion of this vessel type. Following a detailed overview of its research history, he covers all the important issues in the research of the tall-necked, flat-handled jugs: manufacturing techniques and workshops, classification, chronology, typological development, origins and function. Chkhaidze argued that despite the lack of conclusive evidence that the jugs had been produced in Tmutarakan, their presence is attested from the seventh to the mid-eleventh century on the site.[246]

Fabric and tempering agents

The tall-necked, flat-handled jugs made from finely levigated clay tempered with sand or pyroxene were fired to an orange-reddish colour. The jugs were turned on a fast wheel. With the exception of a single exemplar (No. 61), all the jugs from Sinop were tempered with pyroxene, and the use of the same tempering agent was noted among the jugs from Tmutarakan and Chersonesus;[247] in contrast, the sand-tempered, unevenly fired pieces among the jugs brought to light at Sarkel were probably locally made pieces that could be easily distinguished from the others.[248] Antonova identified jugs tempered with mica fired to a brick red colour in the ceramic inventory from Chersonesus (Type 4).[249] The jugs in the collection of the Sinop museum were all fired to an even orange or greyish-red colour, most ranging between 5 YR 6/3 and 7.5 YR 6.4 on the Munsell scale. Most are dull orange or light reddish-brown (5 YR 6/3, four pieces), orange (5 YR 6/6, three pieces) or dull orange (7.5 YR 6/4, two pieces). Vessel colour played a prominent role in the classification system proposed by Antonova and her colleagues: Type 1 was represented by brick red and reddish-brown vessels, Type 2 by orange and

244 Антонова et al. 1971, 91–92, Рис. 20–21.

245 Романчук – Сазанов – Седикова 1995, 63–65, Табл. 30–32; Sazanov 1997, 97, Fig. 4/44.

246 Чхаидзе 2008, 161–173.

247 Плетнева 1963, 54; Антонова et al. 1971, 92.

248 Плетнева 1959, 249.

249 Антонова et al. 1971, 92.

brownish vessels, Type 4 by brick red vessels, while the jugs assigned to Type 3 were poorly fired vessels whose colour could not be determined.[250] No sub-groups could be distinguished on the basis of the tempering agent and vessel colour in the Sinop material.

Formal classification

The jugs assigned to this type were all turned on a fast wheel. They have a short rim with a circumferential groove, a tall cylindrical or slightly funnel-shaped, conical neck, a wide, flat strap handle, an oval body and a flat base. They are fairly tall, standing 40–60 cm high, their rim is narrow, with a diameter rarely exceeding 10 cm, and they have a tall, slender neck. Their capacity ranges between 6 and 8 litres.

Earlier, the classification of formal sub-types was based on the size and proportion of the jugs, which was occasionally combined with the type of tempering agent used in their manufacture and their colour. Pletneva distinguished eighth–ninth-century and tenth–eleventh-century jugs in the material from Tmutarakan based on the size and dimensions of the jugs. The jugs used in the eighth–ninth centuries had a rim diameter of 6–8 cm, while the proportion between the rim diameter, the shoulder diameter and the base diameter was 1:3:2, and the proportion between the rim-shoulder and the vessel height was 1:3. These dimensions and proportions changed by the tenth–eleventh centuries: rim diameters increased to 10–12 cm, and the proportions to 1:2:1 and 1:2–2.5, respectively.[251]

Antonova and her colleagues identified four variants among the jug-amphorae from Chersonesus based on fabric and the jugs' size and wall thickness: (1) tall, slender jugs made from clay tempered with sand fired to a brick red or reddish-brown colour (H. 55 cm, neck diam. 7 cm, belly diam. 19 cm, base diam. 10 cm); (2) large, short-necked, thin-walled jugs with globular belly fired to a bright orange or brown colour with a neck diameter of 13 cm (H. 48 cm, neck diam. 13 cm, belly diam. 24–26 cm, base diam. 12 cm); (3) slender, elongated, poorly fired, thick-walled jugs fired to a greyish colour which lacked a black residue from pitch in their interior.[252]

---

[250] Антонова et al. 1971, 91–92.

[251] Плетнева 1963, 54.

[252] Антонова et al. 1971, 91–92, Рис. 20–21.

Romanchuk, Sazanov and Sedikova assigned the long-necked, flat-handled Chersonesus jugs to their Class 41 and distinguished three types. Type 1 was typical for the occupation levels dated to the last third of the tenth century and earlier eleventh century. Two sub-types could be identified based on the number of handles (one or two). The jugs assigned to Type 2 dated from the earlier eleventh century, while the dating of Type 3 remained controversial.[253] In his comprehensive study on the late antique and early medieval amphorae of the northern Black Sea littoral, Sazanov assigned the long-necked jugs to his Type 44.[254] However, Chkhaidze argued that the earlier classifications and terminology were inaccurate, and that the typological sequence was not sufficiently detailed. He distinguished eight variants based on formal traits, namely the proportions, the dimensions and, in part, the ornamentation of the jugs.[255]

Only two main groups can be distinguished in terms of size and proportions among the jugs in the Sinop museum. The proportion of the exterior rim diameter, the greatest belly diameter and the base diameter could only be determined in the case of five vessels, given that the rim of most jugs was fragmentary. In the case of three jugs (Nos 51, 53, 57), the proportions of the rim diameter, the greatest belly diameter and the base diameter were strikingly similar (1:2.33:1.4) and compare well with the proportions of the late, tenth–eleventh-century jugs from Tmutarakan as determined by Pletneva,[256] which correspond to Types VII and VIII in Chkhaidze's typological scheme.[257] The overall appearance of the jugs with fragmentary rim is highly similar to his Type V.

The jugs' height ranges between 44 and 62 cm, their rim diameter between 8.7 and 13.5 cm, the greatest neck diameter between 5.5 and 9.6 cm, while the greatest diameter between 16.8 and 35.5 cm. They had a capacity of 6–8 litres.

Ornamentation

All the jugs assigned to this type in the Sinop museum were ornamented. The most frequent decoration was a bundle of four lightly incised lines encircling the shoulder above the lower handle attachment. The 2–3 mm wide lines were incised before firing and before the attachment of the handle. This pattern occurred on all vessels, although sometimes there was a single line only (Nos 54–55); both

[253] Романчук – Сазанов – Седикова 1995, 63–65, Табл. 30–32.

[254] Sazanov 1997, 97, Fig. 4/44.

[255] Чхаидзе 2008, 167.

[256] Плетнева 1963, 54.

[257] Чхаидзе 2008, 168, Рис. 91.

jugs were purchased from Ali Arslan, a local fisherman, according to whom he had found them in Kuşlucaköy near Trabzon, suggesting that they came from the same site.

The second most frequently ornamented vessel region is the neck: one to six parallel incised lines on the neck, opposite the upper handle attachment. There are usually one or three incised lines (on six and three amphorae, respectively). Only two jugs among the examined vessels had a plain neck (Nos 56, 62). Most vessels are ornamented on both the neck and the shoulder, while one vessel (No. 55) bears oblique incisions made with a sharp tool, perhaps a knife.

Handles are decorated to a lesser extent. On two jugs (Nos 54, 57), the fan-like widening of the lower handle attachment was accentuated by a thumb-drawn groove. Both jugs come from Kuşlucaköy. Another jug (No. 51) has two rows of punctates, probably impressed with a needle, while another one (No. 59) was perforated, probably with a needle, in two spots down the handle's centre before firing. Punctates impressed on the handles in vertical rows can be noted on the jugs from Sarkel[258] and Partenit in the Crimea.[259] One jug in the Sinop material (No. 58) has a rarely encountered ornamentation of a line incised with a sharp tool encircling the vessel body 1 cm above the base.

Origin and distribution

Several theories have been proposed regarding the origins of this jug type. Early Soviet scholarship assumed a general (northern) Black Sea (*Причерноморье*) origin;[260] however, in the 1950s, the possible local manufacture of certain jugs in Sarkel was proposed on the basis of the large amount of sand used as a tempering agent and their uneven firing.[261] Later, the abundance of the type on the Tmutarakan site led to suggestions that the jugs had been produced on the Taman Peninsula (Tamatarkha/Tmutarakan),[262] despite the lack of workshop finds on the site. The assessment of the pottery from Chersonesus raised the possibility that this ware had been produced in a few central workshops, for example in the town

---

258 Плетнева 1959, 249.

259 Паршина – Созник 2012, 13, Рис. 7.

260 Ляпушкин 1941, 207; Якобсон 1951, 337–338; Якобсон 1979, 43; Плетнева 1959, 251.

261 Якобсон 1951, 337–338; Якобсон 1979, 43; Плетнева 1959, 251; Герцен – Науменко 2001, 135; Сорочан 2005, 1171.

262 Плетнева 1963, 54; Чхаидзе 2008, 161–162.

of Chersonesus itself.[263] The single previously published jug from Sinop was believed to originate from Colchis.[264]

The distinctive pyroxene temper in the fabric of the jugs was neglected in discussions on the origins of the tall-necked, flat-handled jugs, despite the fact that this temper was a hallmark of the amphorae produced in the workshops of Sinope from the Hellenistic period to the end of late antiquity (seventh century). This tempering agent was used in the production of all household pottery between the third century BC and the seventh century AD, not only of amphorae.[265] Given this circumstance and the geology of the middle stretch of the southern Black Sea coast,[266] it is possible that these jugs had been produced in this region too.

Tall-necked, flat-handled jugs were principally distributed on the northern Black Sea coast, on the Crimean and Taman Peninsulas, on urban and rural settlements alike. This jug type has been found on sites of the Don region variant of the Saltovo-Maiak culture, thus, for instance, in the Sarkel fort.[267] It has been recovered from ninth–eleventh-century shipwrecks, such as the one found off the Plaka promontory in the Crimea and on the first Novy Svet wreck.[268] Until recently, jugs were not known from the southern basin of the Black Sea.[269] In their publication of a private collection of amphorae from Sinop, French scholars correctly dated one of the vessels in the material,[270] although they appear to have remained unaware of the typical Black Sea distribution of the type. In addition to the fourteen pieces in the Sinop museum, comparable jugs can be found in the collection of the Samsun and Ordu museums[271] and in the Trabzon area (Kuşlucaköy) on the south-eastern Black Sea coast, indicating that the distribution of these jugs was far more extensive than earlier believed (see *Map 3*).

---

[263] Антонова et al. 1971, 91–92; Романчук 1976, 28.

[264] Kassab Tezgör – Lemaitre – Piéri 2003, 184.

[265] Doonan 2004, 80, 97–119.

[266] Tylecote 1981.

[267] Чхаидзе 2008, 169–170.

[268] Morozova – Albertson 2012, 209, 211.

[269] Sazanov 1997, 97. Citing Hayes 1992, Fig. 21/3, Fig. 40/41, Fig. 42/41, Fig. 63/6 and Fig. 71/53, he claimed that jugs of this type had also been brought to light during the excavations at Saraçhane in Istanbul, but comparable jugs cannot be found among the published finds, and neither have any pieces been brought to light during the recent excavations in the Theodosian Harbour (Yenikapı) (Emre Öncü's kind personal communication).

[270] Kassab Tezgör – Lemaitre – Piéri 2003, 184.

[271] I saw jugs that could be assigned to this type exhibited at these museum during my visit in summer 2011.

Chronology

Although tall-necked, flat-handled jugs were dated to the eighth–eleventh centuries from the initial period of their research,[272] there are major differences between the chronological schemes proposed by individual scholars and the dating of particular sites. The appearance of this jug type was dated to the eighth century at both Tmutarakan and Chersonesus;[273] more recently, Chkhaidze argued that it was current from the seventh century on the Taman Peninsula.[274] It remains uncertain for how long these jugs were used. The finds from Tmutarakan and Chersonesus suggest that funnel-necked jugs can be traced up to the eleventh century,[275] although Sazanov has argued that their continuous use can be attested until the early twelfth century.[276] However, Chkhaidze claimed that the type was only current until the mid-eleventh century on the Taman Peninsula.[277]

Function

Regarding their function, these vessels were used as transport vessels, a function suggested also by the 6–8 litre capacity, their handle that made them suitable for stringing together and their relatively narrow, roughly 10 cm wide rim, which was probably sealed with a stopper during use. The question of what was transported in these vessels is a more controversial issue because there are no graffiti or *dipinti* referring to their contents.

The presence of a black pitch- or resin-like residue inside the vessels was already noted in the 1950s; Liapushkin described this residue as originating from pine resin, citing the results of the analyses performed in the laboratory of the Institute of the History of Material Culture in Leningrad.[278] Pletneva too noted that some 80% of the jugs from Tmutarakan had an interior covered with a black pitch- or resin-like residue, which she too described as pine resin on the testimony of the analyses.[279] Kostrin's chemical analyses in the 1960s yielded significant

---

[272] Якобсон 1951, 337–338; Якобсон 1979, 32–33; Плетнева 1963, 54; Антонова et al. 1971, 91–92.

[273] Плетнева 1963, 54; Антонова et al. 1971, 91–92.

[274] Чхаидзе 2008, 164.

[275] Плетнева 1963, 54.

[276] Sazanov 1997, 97.

[277] Чхаидзе 2008, 164.

[278] Ляпушкин 1941, 207.

[279] Плетнева 1963, 52; Антонова et al. 1971, 92; earlier eleventh century: Романчук – Сазанов – Седикова 1995, 63–65, Табл. 30–32.

new results: he found that the black substance not only covered the surface of the vessel fragments, but had imbued the ceramic fabric as well. The luminescence analysis of the solution extracted from three vessel fragments revealed that the vessels had contained petroleum poor in paraffin. Kostrin quoted Constantine Porphyrogenitus' account of the petroleum deposits on the Taman Peninsula and suggested that the exploitation of these deposits and the trade in petroleum had been principally conducted by the town of Tmutarakan and that the jugs had been used for transporting this commodity.[280]

Chkhaidze raised new points regarding the interpretation of the black residue. Quoting the findings of Kostrin and Anfimov that the black residue found in the interior of the jugs came from petroleum (naphtha) as well as Liapushkin's analytical data from the 1930s, he rejected the possibility that the black residue covering the vessel interiors originated from petroleum in every case, and pointed out that vessels used for transporting liquids were always coated with some substance, usually vegetal resin, to ensure water-tightness. He also noted that the neck of the vessels was often broken, possibly reflecting their opening after they had been sealed.[281]

Another piece of evidence regarding the possible contents comes from Chersonesus, where fifty jugs were found in a storeroom uncovered in Trench XVII of the northern area. These jugs had contained anchovies,[282] indicating that these vessels had probably also been used for transporting a variety of other goods such wine, petroleum and fish.

Catalogue

51. Jug *(Plate 51)*
Inv. no. 1.6.89
Reg. no. 2905
Find context: purchase from fisherman Şükrü Gümüş, resident of Sinop (August 18, 1989)
Pink (5 YR 7/4), well-fired, one-handled jug tempered with fine-grained pyroxene, turned on a fast wheel; clear ringing tone when tapped. Straight, thickened rim with a circumferential groove, the upper part plain and rounded, but angular at the groove; tall, slightly funnel-shaped conical neck; oval upper body tapering into a conical lower part; smooth, flat base. The wide, flat strap handle springs from halfway down the neck to the shoulder, with the lower handle attachment at the greatest diameter. The lower

[280] Кострин 1967, 285–289.
[281] Чхаидзе 2008, 169–170.
[282] Якобсон 1950, 155, Рис. 91.

handle attachment widens fan-like. The handle exterior is flat, the underside is uneven; the exterior is decorated with five pairs of punctates. Three wide incised lines encircle the neck and there are three parallel incised lines around the shoulder. There is a black residue on the rim interior.
H. 47.5 cm, rim diam. 9.3 cm (ext.), 7.8 cm (int.), rim Th. 0.8 cm, rim H. 0.95 cm, Th. 0.6 cm, neck H. 10.8 cm, neck diam. 6.1–9.1 cm, belly diam. 21 cm, base diam. 13 cm, handle H. 11.5 cm, handle W. 5.5–4.2–7.7 cm, handle Th. 1.4–1.8 cm, incised line W. 0.4 cm

52. Jug *(Plate 52)*
Inv. no. 2.9.83
Reg. no. 2555
Find context: purchase from fisherman Ali Arslan, resident of Kuşlucaköy, Trabzon (September 7, 1983)
Light reddish-brown (5 YR 6/3), well fired, one-handled jug tempered with fine-grained pyroxene, turned on a fast wheel; clear ringing tone when tapped. Broken rim; funnel-shaped, conical neck; oval upper body tapering into a conical lower body; smooth, flat base. The wide strap handle springs from the lower third of the neck to the shoulder, with the lower handle attachment at the greatest diameter. The lower handle attachment widens fan-like. The handle exterior is slightly convex with a triangular-sectioned groove down its centre, the underside is flat. An incised line encircles the neck at the upper handle attachment. There are three parallel incised lines around the shoulder. The interior is covered with a black residue, most likely pitch.
H. 44 cm, Th. 0.75–0.9 cm, neck H. 6.3 cm, neck diam. 5.5–6.5 cm, belly diam. 21.5 cm, base diam. 11.2 cm, handle H. 9.5 cm, handle W. 4.6–4.1–5.5 cm, handle Th. 1.3–17 cm

53. Jug *(Plate 53)*
Inv. no. 3.7.90
Reg. no. 2949
Find context: from the Black Sea, purchase from fisherman Şükrü Gümüş, resident of Sinop (Yenimahalle, Vali sokak)
Reddish-yellow (7.5 YR 7/6), well-fired, one-handled jug tempered with fine-grained pyroxene, turned on a fast wheel; clear ringing tone when tapped. Angular, thickened rim with a triangular-sectioned circumferential groove, the rim projects beyond the neck by some 0.45 cm; long, cylindrical neck; oval upper part, cylindrical lower part and flat base. The wide, flat strap handle with convex outer side and flat underside springs from halfway down the neck to the shoulder, attaching at the vessel's greatest diameter; the lower handle attachment expands fan-like. The neck and the shoulder are decorated with incised lines: three roughly parallel, 0.3 cm wide lines on the neck and four roughly parallel lines on the shoulder. The exterior and interior are covered with marine sediment.

H. 62 cm, rim diam. 9.4 cm (ext.), 7.8 cm (int.), rim Th. 0.95 cm, rim H. 1.3 cm, neck H. 17 cm, neck diam. 6.55–8.7 cm, belly diam. 21 cm, base diam. 12.9 cm, handle H. 12 cm, handle W. 5.3–4.6–7 cm, handle Th. 1.2–1.7 cm

54. Jug *(Plate 54)*
Inv. no. 4.1.1982
Reg. no. 2391
Find context: purchase from fisherman Ali Arslan, resident of Kuşlucaköy, Trabzon (November 24, 1982)
Light brown (7.5 YR 6/4), well-fired, one-handled jug tempered with fine-grained sand and pyroxene, turned on a fast wheel; clear ringing tone when tapped. Slightly everted, thickened, lentil-sectioned rim; funnel-shaped neck; oval upper part, tapering conical lower part and smooth, flat base. The wide, flat strap handle with slightly convex exterior and flat underside springs from halfway down the neck to the shoulder, attaching at the greatest diameter. There is a wide, thumb-drawn groove at the lower handle attachment. The neck is encircled by three, 0.4 cm wide incised lines, the shoulder by lightly incised lines. Patches of a black residue (pitch) cover the rim interior.
H. 48.5 cm, Th. 0.85 cm, rim diam. 8.7 cm (ext.), 7.5 cm (int.), rim Th. 1 cm, rim H. 1.5 cm, neck H. 12 cm, neck diam. 5.9–8.3 cm, belly diam. 22 cm, base diam. 11.8 cm, handle H. 11 cm, handle W. 5.3–4.5–5 cm, handle Th. 1.1–1.9 cm

55. Jug *(Plate 55)*
Inv. no. 4.3.1982
Reg. no. 2393
Find context: purchase from fisherman Ali Arslan, resident of Kuşlucaköy, Trabzon (November 24, 1982)
Light reddish-brown (5 YR 6/3), well-fired, one-handled jug tempered with fine-grained pyroxene, turned on a fast wheel; clear ringing tone when tapped. Broken rim; cylindrical neck accounting for a third of the vessel body; oval body tapering into conical lower part and smooth, flat base. The flat, wide strap handle with grooved, slightly convex exterior and flat underside springs from the base of the neck to the shoulder, attaching at the greatest diameter. Both the upper and the lower handle attachment expand fan-like. There is a 0.3 cm wide incised line around the neck at it base, at the upper handle attachment, and a similar line encircles the shoulder at the lower handle attachment. There are four leftward slanting incisions, each roughly 1 cm long, between the two incised lines. A horizontal incision can be found on the vessel base.
H. 50.5 cm, Th. 0.6 cm, neck H. 16 cm, neck diam. 7.9–8.25 cm, belly diam. 22 cm, base diam. 7.8 cm, handle H. 10.5 cm, handle W. 4.9–4.6–6.8 cm, handle Th. 0.9–1.3 cm

56. Jug *(Plate 56)*
Inv. no. 4.6.1982
Reg. no. 2396
Find context: purchase from fisherman Ali Arslan, resident of Kuşlucaköy, Trabzon (November 24, 1982)
One-handled jug tempered with fine-grained pyroxene and small-grained lime, fired to pale yellow (2.5 YR 7/4) on the neck and light brown (7.5 YR 6/4) on the belly; well fired, turned on a fast wheel. Broken rim; the funnel-like neck accounts for a third of the vessel body; the upper part is oval, the lower part is conical; the base is flat without any indication of a foot-ring. The flat, wide strap handle with a barely prominent rib and a concave underside springs from the middle of the neck to the shoulder, attaching at the greatest diameter. Both the upper and the lower handle attachment expand fan-like. There are four 0.45 cm wide incised lines around the shoulder.
H. 47 cm, Th. 0.65–0.8 cm, neck H. 13.5 cm, neck diam. 5.8–7.2 cm, belly diam. 16.8 cm, base diam. 9 cm, handle H. 12 cm, handle W. 5.4–4.6–7 cm, handle Th. 1.45–1.8

57. Jug *(Plate 57)*
Inv. no. 4.7.1982
Reg. no. 2397
Find context: purchase from fisherman Ali Arslan, resident of Kuşlucaköy, Trabzon (November 24, 1982)
Reddish-yellow (5 YR 6/6), well-fired, one-handled jug tempered with fine-grained pyroxene, turned on a fast wheel; clear ringing tone when tapped. Straight, thickened, rounded rim with a circumferential groove; funnel-like neck, accounting for less than a third of the vessel body; the upper part is oval, the lower part tapers into a conical form; smooth, flat base. The flat, wide strap handle with a finger impression in the middle, a slightly convex exterior and a flat underside springs from the lower third of the neck to the shoulder, attaching at the greatest diameter. The lower handle attachment expands fan-like. There is a 0.45 cm wide horizontal incised line around the neck at the upper handle attachment and four parallel 0.35 cm wide incised lines encircle the shoulder. A black residue covers the rim interior.
H. 49 cm, rim diam. 9 cm (ext.), 7.7 cm (int.), rim Th. 0.8–0.9 cm, rim H. 1.6 cm, neck H. 13.5 cm, neck diam. 5.8–8.5 cm, belly diam. 21.5 cm, base diam. 12.1 cm, handle H. 13 cm, handle W. 5.3–4.7–7.8 cm, handle Th. 1.2–1.7 cm

58. Jug *(Plate 58)*
Inv. no. 4.12.83
Reg. no. 2569
Find context: purchase from Durmuş Semir, resident of Sinop (Yenimahalle, Gazhane yolu) (July 6, 1983)

Reddish-brown (5 YR 6/3), well-fired, one-handled jug tempered with fine-grained sand and pyroxene, turned on a fast wheel; clear ringing tone when tapped. Broken rim; slightly funnel-shaped neck accounting for less than a third of the vessel body; oval upper part tapering into a conical lower part; smooth, flat base. The flat, wide strap handle with convex exterior and flat underside springs from the base of the neck to the shoulder, attaching at the greatest diameter. The lower handle attachment expands fan-like. There is an oblique incised line on the neck; the shoulder is encircled by lightly incised lines. A pattern of incised horizontal lines covers the lower part.
H. 50 cm, Th. 0.8 cm, neck H. 10.2 cm, neck diam. 5.8 cm, belly diam. 21 cm, base diam. 10.1 cm, handle H. 13 cm, handle W. 4.6–4.9–4.8 cm, handle Th. 1.6–1.7 cm

59. Jug *(Plate 59)*
Inv. no. 8.5.83
Reg. no. 2586
Find context: purchase from fisherman Kadır Kılıç, resident of Sinop (June 24, 1983)
Reddish-yellow (5 YR 6/6), well-fired, one-handled jug tempered with fine-grained sand and pyroxene, turned on a fast wheel; clear ringing tone when tapped. Broken rim; funnel-like neck accounting for less than a third of the vessel body; oval upper part tapering into a conical lower part; smooth, flat base. The flat, wide strap handle with slightly convex exterior, flat underside and two holes spaced 6.7 cm apart down the centre springs from the middle of the neck to the shoulder, attaching at the greatest diameter. The lower handle attachment expands fan-like. A 0.4 cm wide incised line encircles the neck in line with the upper handle attachment; there are two parallel, deeply incised lines set 0.5 cm apart around the shoulder. The exterior and the interior are covered with marine sediments.
H. 48.5 cm, Th. 0.9 cm, neck H. 12.5 cm, neck diam. 6.3–7.2 cm, belly diam. 19.8 cm, base diam. 10.2 cm, handle H. 12.5 cm, handle W. 4.9–4.3–6 cm, handle Th. 1.3–1.7 cm

60. Jug *(Plate 60)*
Inv. no. 8.99.71
Find context: from the museum's old collection, originally housed in the Pervane madrasah
One-handled jug tempered with fine-grained sand and pyroxene, fired pink (5 YR 7/3) on the belly and light reddish-brown (5 YR 6/3) on the belly; well-fired, turned on a fast wheel; clear ringing tone when tapped. Broken rim; cylindrical neck, accounting for less than a third of the vessel body; oval upper part tapering into a strongly constricted conical lower part; smooth, flat base. The flat, wide strap handle with slightly convex exterior and slightly concave underside springs from the base of the neck to the shoulder, attaching at the greatest diameter. The lower handle attachment expands fan-like. Two more or less parallel lines encircle the neck in line with the upper handle attachment; there are three incised, 0.3 cm wide parallel incised lines spaced 2–3 cm apart around the shoulder.
H. 62 cm, Th. 0.5 cm, neck H. 17 cm, neck diam. 8.1 cm, belly diam. 22.5 cm, base diam. 11.1 cm, handle H. 11 cm, handle W. 6.4–5–9.1 cm, handle Th. 1.2–1.3 cm

61. Jug *(Plate 61)*
Inv. no. 24.4.77
Find context: Sinop, from the Sanctuary of Diogenes, US radar station
Reddish-brown (5 YR 5/3), well-fired, one-handled jug tempered with fine-grained sand, turned on a fast wheel; clear ringing tone when tapped. Straight, rounded rim with a circumferential groove, the upper part is not thickened; slightly funnel-shaped neck accounting for less than a third of the vessel body; oval upper part with strongly tapering towards the base; smooth, plain base. The flat, wide strap handle with slightly convex exterior and flat underside springs from the middle of the neck to the shoulder, attaching at the greatest diameter. The lower handle attachment expands fan-like. The neck is encircled by six parallel incised lines, the shoulder by a pair of incised lines. Marine sediments cover the vessel body in some spots.
H. 61.5 cm, rim diam. 13.5 cm (ext.), 11.2 cm (int.), rim Th. 1.3 cm, rim H. 1.6 cm, neck H. 5 cm neck diam. 9.6–12 cm, belly diam. 35.5 cm, base diam. 15.5 cm, handle H. 14 cm, handle W. 7.4–6.2–11 cm, handle Th. 1.7–2 cm

62. Jug *(Plate 62)*
Inv. no. 35.8.80
Reg. no. 2307
Find context: purchase from Nurettin Saral (January 15, 1981)
Reddish-yellow (5 YR 6/6), well-fired, one-handled jug tempered with fine-grained sand and pyroxene, turned on a fast wheel; clear ringing tone when tapped. Broken rim; cylindrical neck accounting for less than a third of the vessel body; oval upper part tapering into a conical lower part; smooth, flat base. The flat, wide strap handle with smooth exterior and barely prominent rib down the centre of the underside springs from the middle of the neck to the shoulder, attaching at the greatest diameter. The lower handle attachment expands fan-like. A bundle of parallel 0.3 cm wide and 1 mm deep incised lines set 0.5–1 cm apart encircle the shoulder above the lower handle attachment. Marine sediment covers the vessel in some spots.
H. 46.5 cm, Th. 1 cm, neck H. 8 cm, neck diam. 6.7 cm, belly diam. 23 cm, base diam. 12.2 cm, handle H. 12.5 cm, handle W. 4.9–4.1–6 cm, handle Th. 1.4–1.9 cm

63. Jug *(Plate 63)*
Inv. no. 11.6.83
Reg. no. 2599
Find context: purchase from Tayfun Güner, resident of Sinop (July 6, 1983)
Red (2.5 YR 5/6), well-fired, thin-walled, one-handled jug tempered with fine-grained sand and some pyroxene, turned on a fast wheel; clear ringing tone when tapped. High, slightly thickened, angular rim with a light circumferential groove; tall, cylindrical neck; oval upper part, the lower part is missing. The flat, wide strap handle with slightly convex exterior and flat underside springs from the lower third of the neck to the shoulder,

attaching at the greatest diameter. The lower handle attachment expands fan-like. An incised line encircles the neck in the lower third; a pair of incised lines encircles the shoulder above and below the lower handle attachment. A black residue, most likely pitch, covers the vessel interior.

H. 44 cm, rim diam. 9.8 cm, neck diam. 7.6 cm, belly diam. 19.8 cm, handle W. 5.8 cm

Conclusion

Maritime networks of long-distance trade represent a major area of interest in studies on late antique and early medieval economic history. The types and quantities of amphorae brought to light during excavations or discovered underwater are among the main indicators used in archaeology for mapping long-distance and large-scale exchange during late antiquity; however, the study of (early) medieval communication began during the past few decades only. The application of network analysis in studies on seaborne trade is a fairly recent development, which was pioneered by Johannes Preiser-Kapeller in his studies.[283]

Following the prosperous centuries of late antiquity both in Mediterranean and Pontic trade, the ensuing period (eighth to tenth centuries) saw substantial transformations in the economy, generally involving the decline of long-distance and large-volume trade and the emergence of local economies of rather short distance and small scale, which also coincided with the social, administrative and political changes leading to the emergence of the Middle Ages. Research on this economic transformation tended to focus mainly on trans-Mediterranean commerce, while Black Sea trade was usually neglected, even though this region became increasingly important for the economy of the Byzantine Empire following the conquests of the early Islamic Caliphate in the eastern Mediterranean.

The study of the late antique and early medieval amphorae in the collection of the Sinop Archaeological Museum shed new light on the long-term trends in the sea trade of the Black Sea. Following the lead of Henri Pirenne, several scholars questioned the continuity of long-distance sea trade after the seventh century. Later, economic histories and studies on the connectivity of this particular period in the Mediterranean began to emphasise that connectivity between distant regions did not cease, but rather became less visible and its scale was reduced.

There has been a growing scholarly interest in the Black Sea as evidenced by book series, international conferences and monographs dedicated to this topic, most of which, however, have a restricted scope in terms of chronology (late antiquity) or geography (the Crimea and the northern Pontic littoral), while the early medieval period of the southern Pontic shore remained largely unexplored, with only a handful of exceptions. The late antique trans-Pontic trade was comparatively well studied due to the excavation of amphora kilns in Sinop and the subsequent work by Dominique Kassab Tezgör.[284]

---

283 See: Preiser-Kapeller – Daim 2015.

284 Kassab Tezgör 2010a; Kassab Tezgör 2010b.

During my museum research in 2013, I examined 124 artefacts, 87 of which were ceramic wares used for transportation, most of which had been found by local fishermen such as Şükrü Gümüş who is better known as Habeş Kaptan in Sinop. Some of these amphorae (fourteen exemplars) have already been studied by Nergis Günsenin, who assigned them to her Type 1.[285] My main focus was on the transformation of the amphorae from the eighth–ninth centuries. I also examined late antique import amphorae, while local "carrot amphorae" which had been previously covered by D. Kassab Tezgör were excluded from this study in order to gain a better understanding of the nature of imports during the fifth–seventh centuries and the connected regions in order to use these data for comparisons of quantities and changing patterns of connectivity. In several cases, the place of manufacture of the amphorae in question could be determined, suggesting long-distance trade.

The number of late antique import amphorae from the Aegean and the eastern Mediterranean is relatively high: ten LR 1 amphorae dated to the fifth-seventh centuries are housed in the museum, while only four exemplars of the Aegean LR 2 amphorae were found around Sinop. At the same time, western Mediterranean, Palestinian and Italian amphorae are entirely lacking in the studied material.

Early medieval amphorae of the eighth–ninth centuries have not been previously identified and have therefore barely been studied. Three main forms could be distinguished. Seven pieces representing the late variant of LR 2 amphora (LR 2C) are housed in the Sinop museum, while eleven Crimean amphorae were found underwater in the region of the city, representing both variants of this ware. The first variant is represented by four exemplars, the second by seven pieces.

Medieval amphorae from Ganos (Günsenin 1) are well represented in the Sinop Archaeological Museum: the collection includes eighteen exemplars of this type. Three major variants are known, of which the first has been dated to the later ninth century, while the second and third essentially have the same form and differ only regarding their dimensions. The two latter variants are assigned to the tenth and eleventh centuries.

A declining tendency in absolute numbers is clearly visible, even though it is not as striking as originally expected. Another tendency is that the geographical origin of these vessels became limited to the basin of Black Sea and the Sea of Marmara by the ninth century. The dominance of Crimean amphorae around Sinop is a reflection of the connections of this region with the northern Black Sea

[285] GÜNSENIN 1990, 21–24.

shore as well as with Constantinople. Sinope was most likely an important stop on this route during the ninth century.

Between the tenth and eleventh centuries, the most popular amphorae were produced in Ganos (located between Gaziköy and Şarköy, near Tekirdağ) on the shore of the Sea of Marmara.[286] These amphorae were identified as transport vessels for the famous Ganos wine during the Middle Ages. Ganos amphorae are widely distributed across an immense geographical area extending from the Black Sea, the eastern Mediterranean and the Aegean to the rivers valleys of the Balkans and Russia, and even as far as Scandinavia. These amphorae have also been found on several underwater sites such as the shipwrecks of Serçe Limanı, Novy Svet and Tekmezar.[287] The identical graffiti on the vessels from Sinop, Tmutarakan and Sarkel are especially striking, suggesting a strong connectivity between these regions.

The probably most interesting type in the ceramic assemblage discussed here is the so-called Tmutarakan-type or long-necked jug with strap handles, which usually occurs in a package together with both Crimean and Ganos amphorae. These vessels are usually made of clay tempered with pyroxene, they have a short rim with a circumferential groove, a tall cylindrical or slightly funnel-shaped conical neck, an oval body and a flat base. These jugs are often decorated with bundles of incised lines around the neck or shoulder, and sometimes with two rows of punctates down the length of the handle. These vessels were first distinguished as a separate ware on the northern shore of the Black Sea in the Crimea and they were recovered in great quantities during the excavations at Tamatarkha/Tmutarakan from the layers of the site's Khazar occupation (ninth to early tenth century) and the Rus period (tenth–eleventh centuries).[288] These vessels have been attested at other sites too, such as Sarkel in the Don region, indicating that these vessels are characteristic of the Pontic variant of the Saltovo-Maiak culture. However, I found no references regarding their appearance on the southern Black Sea shore in the archaeological literature, in which this ware was usually interpreted as a northern Pontic ceramic type. In addition to the specimens in the Sinop museum, several comparable jugs can be found in the museums of Samsun, Giresun and Trabzon too, suggesting that the use of these transport vessels was not restricted to the northern Black Sea coast.

---

[286] Günsenin 1993, 193–195.

[287] See on page 57.

[288] Чхаидзе 2008, 161–173.

Apart from the type's general distribution, there are some other considerations of why the study of these vessels is relevant to studies on the connectivity of the Pontic lands. About 80% of these jugs from Tmutarakan had an interior covered with a black pitch- or resin-like residue, suggesting that they had been filled with petroleum (naphtha). Some of the pieces in the Sinop Archaeological Museum have a similar black layer on their inner surface, indicating a like content or coating. The residue from jugs of this type was analysed by Amfimov and Kostrin: the former found traces of pine resin, while the latter identified petroleum or naphtha residue on the vessels from Tmutarakan.[289] However, the residue on the vessel interior is not always regarded as originating from the amphora's original content since most of these residues come from the substance with which the vessel interior was coated to ensure water-tightness and we know that tar or crude oil was never used for coating wine or olive oil amphorae, or any transport vessels used for storing food.

Although the exploitation of crude oil or naphtha deposits during such an early period might seem somewhat surprising, it must be borne in mind that naphtha deposits are often mentioned in the ninth-century geographical literature of the Abbasid Caliphate, which describes the oil fields in Azerbaijan and Iraq, and naphtha deposits are also mentioned in Byzantine literature. The domestic and foreign policy manual written by, or rather compiled on the order of, Constantine VII Porphyrogenetus between 948 and 952 mentions several crude oil deposits around the Black Sea:

> "Outside the city of Tamatarcha are many wells yielding naphtha.
>
> In Zichia, near the place called Pagi, which is in the region of Papagia and is inhabited by Zichians, are nine wells yielding naphtha, but the oils of the nine wells are not the same colour, some of them being red, some yellow, and some blackish.
>
> There is there yet another spring yielding naphtha, in the village called Chamouch. Chamouch is the name of the man of olden times who founded the village: for this reason that village was called Chamouch. These places are distant from the sea a journey of one day without changing horses.
>
> In the province of Derzene, near the village of Sapikion and the village called Episkopion, is a well yielding naphtha.

---

[289] Ляпушкин 1941, 207; Кострин 1967, 285–289.

> In the province of Tziliapert, below the village of Srechiabarax, there is a well yielding naphtha." (*De Administrando Imperio* 53, 269be, 209 vP, 493–510)

Two of the listed naphtha wells, Tamatarkha (Tmutarakan) and Zikhia (Abkhazia), lie in the immediate vicinity of the Black Sea, while Derzene is identical with Tercan in the province of Erzincan of Turkey, and Tziliapert (Çıldır gölü) probably lies in north-eastern Turkey in the province of Ardahan. It is striking that one of the major wells lies right next to Tmutarakan (a part of the Maikop-Krasnodar oil fields), where most of the Tmutarakan-type jugs bearing tar residue were discovered.

The crude oil deposits listed in the passages on the Chersoniotes, the residents of Chersonesus, were probably taken from an administrative list of resources, suggesting that oil was one of the major resources of the empire. The reason that naphtha was so important to the Byzantine Empire is that it was the main ingredient of Greek fire, the Byzantines' famous incendiary wonder weapon. It seems likely that the Byzantine administration was fully aware of the significance of crude oil resources as a military supply.

In the light of the above, it comes as little surprise that jugs transporting crude oil have been found in the sea in the Sinop area, which was one of the major ports between the Crimea and Constantinople. The easiest way to reach the capital was sailing to Sinope using the currents and then following the shoreline to the Bosporus.

The study of early medieval transport ceramics from Sinop revealed three parallel processes of transformation: (1) the maritime network of Sinop as outlined by the distribution of eighth–ninth-century amphorae had shrunk considerably compared to the late antique period; (2) the number of amphorae from this period decreased, probably reflecting a smaller scale of trade; and (3) most of these transport vessels were made in the Pontic region, principally in the Crimea, while Ganos amphorae (Sea of Marmara) dominated from the end of ninth century onward. This would suggest that the late antique maritime network of the Black Sea did not vanish without a trace – it quite certainly survived, although on a much smaller scale and with a smaller volume.

Abbreviations

diam.	=	diameter
H.	=	height
Th.	=	thickness
W.	=	width

References

ABADIE-REYNAL – SODINI 1992	ABADIE-REYNAL, C. – SODINI, J.-P.: *La céramique paleochrétienne de Thasos (Aliki, Delkos, fouilles anciennes)*. Études Thasiennes XIII. Athens 1992.
AKKAN 1975	AKKAN, E.: *Sinop Yarımadasının Jeomorfolojisi*. Ankara Üniversitesi Dil ve Tarih–Coğrafya Fakültesi Yayınları 261. Ankara 1975.
AKKEMIK 2015	AKKEMIK, U.: *Woods of Yenikapı – Yenikapı batıklarının ahşapları*. Yenikapı Batıkları 2. İstanbul 2015.
ARMSTRONG 2009	ARMSTRONG, P.: Trade in the East Mediterranean in the 8th century. In: Mundell Mango, M. (ed.): *Byzantine trade, 4th–12th centuries: the archaeology of local, regional and international exchange. Papers of the Thirty-eighth Spring Symposium of Byzantine Studies, St John's College, University of Oxford, March 2004*. Society for the Promotion of Byzantine Studies Publications 14. Farnham–Burlington 2009, 157–178.
ARTHUR 1989	ARTHUR, P.: Aspects of Byzantine Economy: An Evaluation of Amphora Evidence from Italy. In: Déroche, V. – Spieser, J.-M. (eds): *Recherches sur la céramique byzantine*. Bulletin de Correspondance Hellénique Supplement 18 (1989) 79–93.
ARTHUR 1993	ARTHUR, P.: Early Medieval Amphorae, the Duchy of Naples and the Food Supply of Rome. *Papers of the British School at Rome* 61 (1993) 231–244.
ARTHUR 1998	ARTHUR, P.: Eastern Mediterranean amphorae between 500 and 700: a view from Italy. In: Sagui, L. (ed.): *Ceramica in Italia: VI–VII secolo*. Firenze 1998, 157–184.

BASS et al. 2004	BASS, G. F. – MATTHEWS, S. D. – STEFFY, J. R. – VAN DOORNINCK, F. H., JR.: *Serçe Limanı: An Eleventh-Century Shipwreck. Vol. I. The Ship and its Anchorage, Crew, and Passengers*. College Station (TAMU) 2004.
BALLANCE et al. 1989	BALLANCE, M. – BOARDMAN, J. – CORBETT, S. – HOOD, S.: *Excavations in Chios 1952–1955: Byzantine Emporio*. British School of Athens, Supplement 20. Oxford 1989.
BASS – VAN DOORNINCK 1982	BASS, G. F. – VAN DOORNINCK, F. H.: *Yassi Ada I. A Seventh-century Shipwreck*. College Station (TAMU) 1982.
BELKE 1996	BELKE, K.: *Paphlagonien und Honōrias*. Tabula Imperii Byzantini 9. Wien 1996.
BIKIĆ – IVANIŠEVIĆ 2012	BIKIĆ, V. – IVANIŠEVIĆ, V.: Imported pottery in central Illyricum – A case study: Caričin Grad (Iustiniana Prima). *Acta Rei Cretariae Romanae Fautores* 42 (2012) 41–49.
BJELAJAC 1996	BJELAJAC, L.: *Amfore gornjo mezijskog Podunavlja*. Beograd 1996.
BÖTTGER 1974	BÖTTGER, B.: Die Importkeramik aus dem spätantiken Donaulimeskastell Iatrus in Nordbulgarien. In: Pippidi, D. M. (ed.): *Actes du IXe Congrès International d'Études sur les Frontières Romaines*. Bucharest–Cologne–Vienne 1974, 131–136.
BÖTTGER 1982	BÖTTGER, B.: Die Gefässkeramik aus dem Kastell Iatrus. In: Böttger, B. (ed.): *Iatrus-Krivina: Spätantike Befestigung und frühmittelalterliche Siedlung an der unteren Donau 2. Ergebnisse der Ausgrabungen 1966–1973*. Berlin 1982, 33–148.
BÖTTGER 1990	BÖTTGER, B.: Zur Lebensmittelversorgung des niedermösischen Kastells Iatrus (4–6. Jh.). In: Vetters, H. – Kandler, M. (Hrsg.): *Akten des 14. internationalen Limeskongresses 1986 in Carnuntum*. Wien 1990, 925–930.

BÖTTGER 1991 — BÖTTGER, B.: Die gefäßkeramischen Funde (1975-1981). In: Wachtel, K. (Hrsg.): *Iatrus-Krivina: Spätantike Befestigung und frühmittelalterliche Siedlung an der unteren Donau 4.* Ergebnisse der Ausgrabungen 1975-1981. Berlin 1991, 157–166.

BRYER – WINFIELD 1985 — BRYER, A. – WINFIELD, D.: *The Byzantine Monuments and Topography of the Pontos.* Dumbarton Oaks Studies 20. Washington D.C. 1985.

CHANDLER – FOX 1974 — CHANDLER, T. – FOX, G.: *3000 Years of Urban Growth.* New York 1974.

CONDURACHI et al. 1954 — CONDURACHI, E. – PIPPIDI, D.M. – BORDENACHE, G. – STOIAN, I. – DIMITRIU, S. – RADU, C. – ZIRRA, V. – COJA, M. – EFTIMIE, V. – ALEXANDRESCU, P.: *Histria. Monografie arheologica* I. Bucureşti, 1954.

CURTA 2004 — CURTA, F.: *The Making of the Slavs. History and Archaeology of the Lower Danube Region c. 500–700.* Cambridge 2004.

CSIKY 2012 — CSIKY, G.: The Pontus region from a new perspective: research on the early medieval contacts of Sinope. *Hungarian Archaeology* (autumn 2012) 1–7. Available online at http://www.hungarianarchaeology.hu/wp-content/uploads/2012/11/eng_CsikyG_pontusvidek_12OK.pdf (last accessed March 16, 2016).

CSIKY 2015 — CSIKY, G.: Sinope in the early medieval economy of the Black Sea region (questions and problems) *Antaeus* 33 (2015) 315–344.

CSIKY – HÁRSHEGYI 2015 — CSIKY, G. – HÁRSHEGYI, P.: Wine for the Avar elite? Amphorae from Avar period burials in the Carpathian Basin. In: Tsetskhladze, G. R. – Avram, A. – Hargrave, J. (eds): *The Danubian Lands between the Black, Aegean and Adriatic Seas (7th Century BC–10th Century AD). Proceedings of the Fifth International Congress on Black Sea Antiquities (Belgrade – 17–22 September 2013).* Oxford 2015, 175–182.

De Graauw 2000	De Graauw, A.: *Port engineering aspects of the Magnus Portus in Alexandria. Bulletin of the Permanent International Association of Navigation Congresses* 103 (2000) 31–41.
De Ligt 2008	De Ligt, L.: The Population of Cisalpine Gaul in the Time of Augustus, in: L. de Ligt – S. J. Northwood (eds): *People, Land and Politics. Demographic Developments and the Transformation of Roman Italy, 300 BC-AD 14*. Mnemosyne Supplements: History and Archaeology of Classical Antiquity 303. Leiden – Boston 2008, 139–183.
Demangel – Mamboury 1939	Demangel, R. – Mamboury, E.: *Le quartier des Manganes et la première region de Constantinople.* Paris 1939.
Demesticha 2000	Demesticha, S.: The Paphos kiln: Manufacturing Techniques of LR1 amphoras. *Acta Rei Cretariae Romanae Fautores* 36 (2000) 549–553.
Demesticha 2003	Demesticha, S.: Amphora production on Cyprus during the Late Roman Period. In: Bakirtzis, C. (ed.): *De Rome à Byzance; de Foustat à Cordoue: évolution des facies céramiques en Méditerranée (Ve–IXe siècles)*. Athen 2003, 469–476.
Demesticha – Michaelides 2001	Demesticha, S. – Michaelides, D.: Excavation of a Late Roman 1 amphora kiln in Paphos. In: Villeneuve, E. – Watson, P. M. (eds): *La céramique byzantine et protoislamique en Syrie-Jordaine (IVe–VIIIe siècles apr. J.-C.)*. Beyrouth 2001, 289–296.
Denker et al. 2013	Denker, A. – Demirkök, F. – Kongaz, G. – Kiraz, M. – Korkmaz Kömürcü, Ö. – Akbaytogan, T.: YK 12. In: *Saklı Limandan hikayeler. Yenikapı'nın batıkları.* İstanbul 2013, 197–209.
Doonan 2004	Doonan, O. P.: *Sinop Landscapes. Exploring Connection in a Black Sea Hinterland.* Philadelphia 2004.

EMPEREUR – PICON 1989 EMPEREUR, J.-Y. – PICON, M.: Les régions de production d'amphores impériales en Méditerranée Orientale. In: *Amphores romaines et historire économique: dix ans de recherche.* Rome 1989, 223–248.

FALKNER 1999 FALKNER, R.: The Pottery. In: Poulter, A. G. (ed.): *Nicopolis ad Istrum: The Finds.* London–Oxford 1999, 55–296.

FERNÁNDEZ FERNÁNDEZ 2012 FERNÁNDEZ FERNÁNDEZ, A.: Datos preliminares sobre las ánforas orientales tardías de dos yacimentos de Vigo (Galicia, Espana), con el ejemplo de un contexto de la primera mitad del s. VII. In: *Rei Cretariae Romanae Fautorum Acta* 42. Bonn 2012, 355–362.

GEDIK – ERCAN – KORKMAZ 1982–83 GEDIK, A. – ERCAN, T. – KORKMAZ, S.: Orta Karadeniz (Samsun-Sinop) havzasının jeolojisi ve volkanik kayaçlarının petrolojisi. *Maden Tetkik ve Arama Dergisi* 99–100 (1982–83) 34–51.

GEDIK – KORKMAZ 1984 GEDIK, A. – KORKMAZ, S.: Sinop havzasının jeolojisi ve petrol olanakları. *Türk Mühendis ve Mimar Odaları Birliği Jeoloji Mühendisliği Odası* (1984) 53–80.

GIARDINI – MURIALDO 1994 GIARDINI, A. – MURIALDO, G.: La Liguria. In: Francovich, R. – Noyé, G. (eds): *La storia dell'alto medioaevo italiano (VI–IX secolo) alla luce dell'archeologia.* Firenze 1994, 170–171.

GRÜNBART – LOCHNER-METAXAS 2002 GRÜNBART, M. – LOCHNER-METAXAS, S.: Stempel(n) in Byzanz. In: Hörandner, W. – Koder, J. – Stassinopoulou, M. (eds): *Wiener Byzantinistik und Neogräzistik. Beiträge zum Symposion 40 Jahre Institut für Byzantinistik und Neogräzistik der Universität Wien im Gedenken an Herbert Hunger. Wien 4.–7. Dezember 2002.* Byzantina et Neograeca Vindobonensia 24. Wien 2004, 177–189.

GÜNSENIN 1989 — GÜNSENIN, N.: Recherches sur les amphores byzantines dans les musées turcs. In: Déroche, V. – Spieser, J.-M. (eds): *Recherches sur la céramique byzantine.* Bulletin de Correspondance Hellénique Supplement 18 (1989) 267–276.

GÜNSENIN 1990 — GÜNSENIN, N.: *Les amphores byzantines (X^{e}–XIIeme siècles): typologie, production, circulation d'après les collections turques*. Thèse doctorat de l'Université de Paris I. Paris 1990.

GÜNSENIN 1993 — GÜNSENIN, N.: Ganos. Centre de production d'amphores à l'époque byzantine. *Anatolia Antiqua* 2 (1993) 193–201.

GÜNSENIN 1995 — GÜNSENIN, N.: Ganos: résultats des campagnes de 1992 et 1993. *Anatolia Antiqua* 3 (1995) 165–178.

GÜNSENIN 1998 — GÜNSENIN, N.: Récentes découvertes sur l'île de Marmara (Proconnèse) à l'époque byzantine [Épaves et lieux de chargement]. In: *Construction navale maritime et fluviale. Approches archéologique, historique et ethnologique. Archaeonautica* 14 (1998) 309–316.

GÜNSENIN 1999 — GÜNSENIN, N.: From Ganos to Serce Limani: Social and economic activities in the Propontis during Medieval Times illuminated by recent archaeological and historical discoveries. *INA Quarterly* 26/3 (1999) 18–23.

GÜNSENIN 2009 — GÜNSENIN, N.: Ganos wine and its circulation in the 11th century. In: Mundell Mango, M. (ed.): *Byzantine trade, 4th–12th centuries: the archaeology of local, regional and international exchange. Papers of the Thirty-eighth Spring Symposium of Byzantine Studies, St John's College, University of Oxford, March 2004.* Society for the Promotion of Byzantine Studies Publications 14. Farnham–Burlington 2009, 145–153.

GÜNSENIN 2012 — GÜNSENIN, N.: Un graffito de bateau à voile latine sur une amphore (IXe s. ap. J.-C.) du *Portus Theodosiacus* (Yenikapı). *Anatolia Antiqua* 20 (2012) 157–164.

GÜNSENIN – HATCHER 1997 — GÜNSENIN, N. – HATCHER, H.: Analyses chimiques comparatives des amphores de Ganos, de l'île de Marmara et de l'épave de Serçe Limanı (Glass-Wreck). *Anatolia Antiqua* 5 (1997) 249–260.

HAUTUMM 1981 — HAUTUMM, W.: *Studien zu Amphoren der spät-römischen und frühbyzantinischen Zeit*. Fulda 1981.

HAYES 1992 — HAYES, J. W.: *Excavations at Saraçhane in Istanbul* II. Princeton 1992.

HOCKER 1998 — HOCKER, F. M.: Bozburun Byzantine shipwreck excavation. The final campaign, 1998. *INA Quarterly* 25/4 (1998) 3–13.

İNANDIK 1955 — İNANDIK, H.: Sinop – Terme arasındaki kıyıların morfolojik etüdü. *Türk Coğrafya Dergisi* XII/15–16 (1955) 21–45.

İNANDIK 1957 — İNANDIK, H.: Sinop – Terme arasındaki kıyıların morfolojik etüdü 2. *Türk Coğrafya Dergisi* XIII/17 (1957) 51–71.

KARAGIORGOU 2001 — KARAGIORGOU, O.: LRA2: a container from the military annona on the Danubian border? In: Kingsley, S. – Decker, M. (eds): *Economy and Exchange in the East Mediterranean during Late Antiquity*. Oxford 2001, 129–166.

KARAGIORGOU 2009 — KARAGIORGOU, O.: Mapping trade by the amphora. In: Mundell Mango, M. (ed.): *Byzantine trade, 4th–12th centuries: the archaeology of local, regional and international exchange. Papers of the Thirty-eighth Spring Symposium of Byzantine Studies, St John's College, University of Oxford, March 2004*. Society for the Promotion of Byzantine Studies Publications 14. Farnham–Burlington 2009, 37–58.

KASSAB TEZGÖR 2010a	KASSAB TEZGÖR, D.: *Les fouilles et le materiel de l'atelier amphorique de Demirci près de Sinope: recueil de travaux*. Varia Anatolica 22. Paris 2010.
KASSAB TEZGÖR 2010b	KASSAB TEZGÖR, D.: Le réseau commercial des amphores sinopéennes entre les IIe–IIIe s. et le VIe s. de notre ère. In: Kassab Tezgör, D. – Inaishvili, N. (eds): *PATABS I. Production and Trade of Amphorae in the Black Sea. Actes de la Table Ronde internationale de Batoumi et Trabzon, 27–29 avril 2006.* Varia Anatolica 21. Istanbul 2010, 167–173.
KASSAB TEZGÖR – LEMAITRE – PIÉRI 2003	KASSAB TEZGÖR, D. – LEMAITRE, S. – PIÉRI, D.: La Collection d'amphores d'İsmail Karakan à Sinop. *Anatolia Antiqua* 11 (2003) 169–200.
KEAY 1984	KEAY, S. J.: *Late Roman amphorae in the western Mediterranean. A typology and economic study: the Catalan evidenc*e. British Archaeological Reports International Series 196. Oxford 1984.
KINGSLEY 2009	KINGSLEY, S.: Mapping trade by shipwrecks. In: Mundell Mango, M. (ed.): *Byzantine trade, 4th–12th centuries : the archaeology of local, regional and international exchange. Papers of the Thirty-eighth Spring Symposium of Byzantine Studies, St John's College, University of Oxford, March 2004.* Society for the Promotion of Byzantine Studies Publications 14. Farnham–Burlington 2009, 31–36.
KIZILTAN – ÇELIK 2013	KIZILTAN, Z. – ÇELIK, G. B.: *Stories From the Hidden Harbor: Shipwrecks of Yenikapı.* Istanbul 2013.
KOCABAŞ 2012	KOCABAŞ, U.: *The 'old ships' of the 'new gate'. Yenikapı'nın eski gemileri.* Yenikapı Batıkları 1. Istanbul 2012.
LADSTÄTTER – PIRSON – SCHMIDTS 2015	LADSTÄTTER, S. – PIRSON, F. – SCHMIDTS, T. (eds): *Harbors and Harbor Cities in the Eastern Mediterranean from Antiquity to the Byzantine Period: Recent Discoveries and Current Approaches. Byzas* 19 (2015)

Lane 1938	Lane, A.: Medieval finds at Al Mina in North Syria. *Archaeologia* 87 (1938) 19–78.
Lightfoot – Lightfoot 2006	Lightfoot, C. S. – Lightfoot, M.: *Amorium: A Byzantine City in Anatolia.* Istanbul 2006.
Mackensen 1987	Mackensen, M.: Mediterrane Sigillata, Lampen und Amphoren. In: Bierbrauer, V.: *Invillino – Ibligo in Friaul 1. Die römische Siedlung und das spätantik-frühmittelalterliche Castrum.* Münchner Beiträge zur Vor- und Frühgeschichte 33. München 1987, 229–265.
Mackensen 1992	Mackensen, M.: Amphoren und Spatheia von Golemanovo Kale. In: Uenze, S.: *Die spätantiken Befestigungen von Sadovec (Bulgarien): Ergebnisse der deutsch-bulgarischen-österreichischen Ausgrabungen 1934–1937.* München 1992, 239–254.
Magdalino 2000	Magdalino, P.: The maritime neighborhoods of Constantinople: Commercial and residential functions, sixth to twelfth centuries. *Dumbarton Oaks Papers* 54 (2000) 209–226.
Mango 1985	Mango, C.: *Le dévelopment urbain de Constantinople (IVe – VIIe siècles).* Travaux et Mémoires du Centre des Recherche d'Histoire et Civilisation de Byzance, Collège de France, Monographies 2. Paris 1985.
Morozova – Albertson 2012	Morozova, I. I. – Albertson, J. A.: Byzantine shipwrecks explored by the centre for underwater archaeology in the Black Sea. In: *1000 років візантійської торгівлі (V–XV століття). Збірка наукових праць.* Бібліотека Vita Antiqua. Київ 2012, 208–212.
Mundell Mango 2000	Mundell Mango, M.: The Commercial Map of Constantinope. *Dumbarton Oaks Papers* 54 (2000) 189–207.
Opaiţ 1996	Opaiţ, A.: *Aspecte ale vieţii economice din provincia Scythia (secolele IV–VI p. Ch.). Producţia ceramicii locale şi de import.* Bucureşti 1996.

OPAIȚ 2004a — OPAIȚ, A.: *Local and Imported Ceramics in the Roman Province of Scythia (4th–6th centuries AD).* British Archaeological Reports International Series 1274. Oxford 2004.

OPAIȚ 2004b — Opaiţ, A.: The Eastern Mediterranean Amphorae in the Province of Scythia. In: Eiring, J. – Lund, J. (eds): *Transport Amphorae and Trade in the Eastern Mediterranean.* Aarhus 2004, 293–308.

OPAIȚ 2010 — OPAIȚ, A.: On the origin of Carthage LR amphora 1. In: Menchelli, S. – Santoro, S. – Pasquinucci, M. – Guiducci, G. (eds): *LRCW3. Late Roman Coarse Wares, Cooking Wares and Amphorae in the Mediterranean: Archaeology and archaeometry. Comparison between western and eastern Mediterranean.* II. British Archaeological Reports International Series 2185. Oxford 2010.

OPRIŞ 2003 — OPRIŞ, I. C.: *Ceramica romană târzie şi paleobizantină de la Capidava în contextul descoperirilor de la Dunărea de Jos (sec. IV.–VI. p. Chr.)* Bucureşti 2003.

ÖZDEMİR 2002 — ÖZDEMİR, N.: *Sinop ilinde doğal afetlerden etkilenen yerleşmeler.* T. C. Ankara Üniversitesi Sosyal Bilimleri Enstitüsü Coğrafya (Türkiye Coğrafyası) Anabilim dalı doktora tezi. Ankara 2002.

ÖZTUNCAY – KARAMANI PEKIN 2007 — ÖZTUNCAY, B. – KARAMANI PEKIN, A. (eds) I*stanbul, 8000 years brought to daylight (Marmaray, Metro Sultanahmet Excavations)* Istanbul 2007.

PAPADOPOULOS 1989 — PAPADOPOULOS, J. K.: Roman amphorae from the excavations at Torone. *Archaiologike Ephemeris* 128 (1989) 67–103.

PAROLI – DELOGU 1993 — PAROLI, L. – DELOGU, P.: *La storia economica di Roma nell'alto medioevo alla luce dei recenti scavi archeologici.* Atti del seminario. Firenze 1993.

PEACOCK 1984 — PEACOCK, D. P. S: Petrology and Origins. In: *Excavations at Carthage: The British Mission,* Vol. 1. *The Avenue du Président Habib Bourguiba, Salammbo: 2. The pottery and other ceramic objects from the site.* Sheffield 1984, 6–28

PEACOCK – WILLIAMS 1986 — PEACOCK, D. P. S. – WILLIAMS, D. F.: *Amphorae and the Roman Economy. An Introductory Guide.* London 1986.

PIÉRI 1998 — PIÉRI, D.: Les importations d'amphores orientales en Gaule méridionale durant l'antiquité tardive et le haut-moyen age (IVe–VIIe siècles après J.-C.): Typologie, chronologie et contenu. *SFECAG, Actes du Congrès d'Istres.* 1998, 97–106.

PIÉRI 2005 — PIÉRI, D.: *Le commerce du vin oriental à l'époque byzantine (Ve–VIIe siècles). Le témoignage des amphores en Gaule.* Bibliothèque archéologique et historique 174. Beyrouth 2005.

PIÉRI 2007 — PIÉRI, D.: Béryte dans le grand commerce méditerranéen. Production et importation d'amphores dans le Levant protobyzantin (Ve–VIIe s. ap. J.-C.). In: Sartre, M. (éd.): *Productions et échanges dans la Syrie gréco-romaine.* Actes du 2e colloque international sur la Syrie antique (Tours, 12–13 juin 2003). Topoi Orient Occident, Supplement 8. Lyon–Paris 2007, 297–327.

POPOVIĆ 1988 — POPOVIĆ, M.: Svetinja, novi podaci o ranovizantijskom Viminaciumu. *Starinar* 38 (1988) 1–37.

POUNDS 2005 — POUNDS, N. J. G.: *The Medieval City.* Greenwood Guides to Historic Events of the Medieval World. Westport 2005.

Preiser-Kapeller – Daim 2015	Preiser-Kapeller, J. – Daim, F. (eds): *Harbours and Maritime Networks as Complex Adaptive Systems.* International Workshop »Harbours and maritime Networks as Complex Adaptive Systems« at the Römisch-Germanisches Zentralmuseum in Mainz, 17.–18.10.2013, within the framework of the Special Research Programme (DFG-SPP 1630) »Harbours from the Roman Period to the Middle Ages« RGZM – Tagungen 23. Interdisziplinäre Forschungen zu den Häfen von der Römischen Kaiserzeit bis zum Mittelalter in Europa 2. Mainz 2015.
Rădulescu 1976	Rădulescu, A.: Amfore romane şi romano-bizantine din Scythia Minor. *Pontica* 9 (1976) 99–114.
Reynolds 1995	Reynolds, P.: *Trade in the Western Mediterranean, AD 400–700: The Ceramic Evidence.* British Archaeological Reports International Series 604. Oxford 1995.
Reynolds 2005	Reynolds, P.: Levantine amphorae from Cilicia to Gaza: a typology and analysis of regional production trends from the 1st to 7th centuries. In: Gurt i Esparraguera, J. M. – Buxeida i Garrigós, J. – Cau Ontiveros, M. A. (eds): *LRCW I: Late Roman Coarse and Cooking Wares and Amphorae in the Mediterranean: Archaeology and Archaeometry.* British Archaeological Reports International Series 1340. Oxford 2005, 563–611.
Riley 1979	Riley, J. A.: The coarse pottery from Berenice. In: Lloyd, J. A.: *Excavations at Sidi Khrebish Benghazi (Berenice). Vol. II.* Supplement to Libya Antiqua 5. London 1979, 91–467.
Riley 1981	The pottery from the cisterns 1977.1, 1977.2, 1977.3. In: Humphrey, J. H. (ed.): *Excavations at Carthage conducted by the University of Michigan.* 6. Ann Arbor 1981, 85–124.

ROBINSON 1959 — ROBINSON, H.: *The Athenian Agora 5. Pottery of the Roman Period. Chronology.* Princeton 1959.

SAZANOV 1997 — SAZANOV, A.: Les amphores de l'Antiquité tardive et du Moyen Age: continuité ou rupture? Le cas de la Mer Noire. In: Démians D'Achimbaud, G. (pub.): *La céramique médiévale en Méditerranée. Actes du VIe congrès de l'AIECM2 Aix-en-Provence (13–18 novembre 1995).* Aix-en-Provence 1997, 87–102.

SAZANOV 1999 — SAZANOV, A.: Les amphores ‹‹LA 1 Carthage›› dans la région de la Mer Noire. (Typologie et chronologie: V^e–VIIe s. apr. J.-C.). In: Garlan, Y. (ed.): *Production et commerce des amphores anciennes en Mer Noire. Colloque international organisé à Istanbul, 25–28 mai 1994, par le GDR 830, avec le concours du CNRS, du GDR 1056, de l'Institut Français d'Études Anatoliennes, du Ministère des Affaires Étrangères et de l'Université de Haute-Bretagne.* Aix-en-Provence 1999, 265–279.

SCHEIDEL 2008 — SCHEIDEL, W.: Roman Population Size: The Logic of the Debate. in: L. de Lig – S. J. Northwood (eds): *People, Land and Politics. Demographic Developments and the Transformation of Roman Italy, 300 BC-AD 14.* Mnemosyne Supplements: History and Archaeology of Classical Antiquity 303. Leiden – Boston 2008, 17–70.

SCORPAN 1976 — Origini şi linii evolutive în ceramica romano-bizantină (sec. IV–VII) din spaţiul mediteranean şi pontic. *Pontica* 9 (1976) 155–185.

SCORPAN 1977 — SCORPAN, C.: Contributions à la connaissance de certains types céramiques romano-byzantins (IVe–VIIe siècles) dans l'espace istro-pontique. *Dacia* N.S. 21 (1977) 269–297.

SEGRÉ 1942–43 — SEGRÉ, A.: Essays on Byzantine Economic History I. The Annona Civica and the Annona Militaris. *Byzantion* 16 (1942-43) 393–444.

SWAN 2004 — SWAN, V. G.: Dichin (Bulgaria) and the supply of amphorae to the Lower Danube in the late Roman-early Byzantine period. In: Eiring, J. – Lund, J. (eds): *Transport Amphorae and Trade in the Eastern Mediterranean.* Aarhus 2004, 371–382.

TARKAN 1941 — TARKAN, H.: *Sinop Coğrafyası.* İzmir 1941.

TOMBER – WILLIAMS 1986 — TOMBER, R. – WILLIAMS, D.: Late Roman amphorae in Britain. *Journal of Roman Pottery Studies* 1 (1986) 42–54.

TOPOLEANU 2000 — TOPOLEANU, F.: *Ceramica romana şi romano-bizantina da la Halmyris (sec. I–VII d. Chr.).* Tulcea 2000.

TÓTH – HORVÁTH 1992 — H. TÓTH, E. – HORVÁTH, A.: *Kunbábony. Das Grab eines Awarenkhagans.* Kecskemét 1992.

TSARAVOPOULOS 1986 — TSARAVOPOULOS, A.: The city of Khios. A contribution to the topography of the city from the results of rescue excavations. *Horos* 4 (1986) 124–144.

TUNA et al. 1987 — TUNA, N. – EMPEREUR, J.-Y. – PICON, M. – DÖĞER, E.: Rapport préliminaire de la prospection archéologique turco-française des ateliers d'amphores de Reşadiye-Kiliseyanı sur la Péninsule de Datça. *Anatolia Antiqua* (1987) 47–52.

TYLECOTE 1981 — TYLECOTE, R. F.: Iron Sands from the Black Sea. *Anatolian Studies* 31 (1981) 137–139.

ÜNAL 2008 — ÜNAL, M. A.: *Osmanlı Devrinde Sinop (XV. Yüzyıldan XVIII. Yüzyıla Sinop Kazâsı).* Isparta 2008.

VAN ALFEN 1996 — VAN ALFEN, P. G.: New light on the 7th-c. Yassı Ada shipwreck: capacities and standard sizes of LRA1. *Journal of Roman Archaeology* 9 (1996) 189–213.

VAN ALFEN 2015 — VAN ALFEN, P. G.: The Restudy of the LR2 Amphoras from the Seventh-Century Yassıada Shipwreck. Preliminary Evidence for Standardization. In: Carlson, D. N. – Leidwanger, J. – Kampbell, S. M. (eds): *Maritime Studies in the Wake of the Byzantine Shipwreck at Yassıada*, Turkey. College Station (TAMU) 2015, 17–34.

VAN DE VORST 1911 — VAN DE VORST, Chr.: Saint Phocas. *Annalecta Bollandiana* 30. 1911. 252–295

VAN DOORNINCK 1989 — VAN DOORNINCK, F. H.: The cargo amphoras on the 7th century Yassı Ada and 11th century Serçe Limanı shipwrecks: two examples of a reuse of Byzantine amphoras as transport jars. In: Déroche, V. – Spieser, J.-M. (eds): *Recherches sur la céramique byzantine.* Bulletin de Correspondance Hellénique Supplement 18 (1989) 247–257.

VAN DOORNINCK 1993 — VAN DOORNINCK, F. H.: Giving Good Weight. In: Eleventh-Century Byzantium: The Metrology of the Glass Wreck Amphoras. *INA Quarterly* 20/2 (1993) 8–12.

VAN DOORNINCK 2002 — VAN DOORNINCK, F. H.: The Byzantine Ship at Serçe Liman: An Example of Small-Scale Maritime Commerce with Fatimid Syria in the Early Eleventh Century. In Macrides, R. (ed.): *Travel in the Byzantine World.* Aldershot 2002, 137–148.

VENEDIKOV 1969 — VENEDIKOV, I.: *Nessebre.* Sofia 1969.

VIDA 1999 — VIDA, T.: *Die awarenzeitliche Keramik I. (6.–7. Jh.).* Varia Archaeologica Hungarica VIII. Berlin–Budapest 1999.

VIONIS – POBLOME – WAELKENS 2009 — VIONIS, A.K. – POBLOME, J. – WAELKENS, M.: The hidden material culture of the Dark Ages. Early medieval ceramics at Sagalassos (Turkey): new evidence (ca. AD 650–800). *Anatolian Studies* 59 (2009) 147–165.

WALMSLEY 2000	WALMSLEY, A.: Production, exchange and regional trade in the Islamic East Mediterranean: old Structures, new Systems? in: Hensen, I. L. – Wickham, C. (eds): *The Long Eighth Century. Production, Distribution and Demand.* Leiden 2000, 265–343.
WILLIAMS 1982	WILLIAMS, D. F.: The petrology of certain amphorae: some suggestions as to origins. In: *Colloque sur la céramique antique. Carthage 23–24 June 1980.* Carthage 1982, 99–110.
ZIMMERMANN MUNN 1985	ZIMMERMANN MUNN, M. L.: A Late Roman kiln site in Hermionid Greece. *American Journal of Archaeology* 89 (1985) 342–343.
АНТОНОВА et al. 1971	АНТОНОВА, И. А. – ДАНИЛЕНКО, В. Н. – ИВАШУТА, Л. П. – КАДЕЕВ, В. И. – РОМАНЧУК, А. И.: Средневековые амфоры Херсонеса. *Античная древность и средние века* 7 (1971) 81–101.
АРТАМОНОВ 1935	АРТАМОНОВ, М. И.: *Средневековые поселения на нижнем Дону по материалам Северо-Кавказской экспедиции.* ИГАИМК 131. Ленинград 1935.
БАРСАМОВ 1926	БАРСАМОВ, Н. С.: Феодосийский музей краеведения. *Крым* 2. Москва 1926.
БЕРДЗЕНИШВИЛИ – ПУТУРИДЗЕ 1975	БЕРДЗЕНИШВИЛИ, К. И. – ПУТУРИДЗЕ, Р. В.: *Пицундские амфоры. / Великий Пициунт.* Тбилиси 1975.
БУЛГАКОВ – ЯКОВЛЕВ 2003	БУЛГАКОВ, В. В. – КРАМАРЕНКО, Н. К. – ЯКОВЛЕВ, Б. Г.: Петрографическая характеристика византийских желтоглиняных вогнутодонных амфор XII–XIII вв. In: *Византийские амфоры:* 15.05.2003 г. Available online at http://archaeology.kiev.ua/byzantine/amphorae/analysis/bulgakov8.htm
ДОНЧЕВА-ПЕТКОВА 1977	ДОНЧЕВА-ПЕТКОВА, Л.: *Българската битова керамика през ранното Средновековие.* София 1977.

Гамбашидзе 1963	Гамбашидзе, О. С.: Бичвинта. Предварительный отчет археологических работ, производимых в 7-м раскопе 1956–57 гг. *Материалы по археологии Грузии и Кавказа* III (1963) 123–129.
Герцен – Науменко 2001	Герцен, А. Г. – Науменко, В. Е.: Керамика IX–XI вв. жилого комплекса на мысе Тешкли-Бурун. *Античная древность и средние века* 32 (2001) 127–147.
Кострин 1967	Кострин, К. В.: Исследования смолистого вещества из «черно-смоленых» кувшинов средневековой Тмутаракани. *Советская Археология* 1967/1, 285–289.
Кузманов 1973	Кузманов, Г.: Типология и хронология на ранновизантийските амфори (IV–VI в.). *Археология* XV/1 (1973) 14–21.
Кузманов 1985	Кузманов, Г.: Ранновизантийска керамика от Тракия и Дакия (IV–началото на VII в.) *Разкопки и Проучвания* 13. София 1985.
Ляпушкин 1941	Ляпушкин, И. И.: *Славяно-русские поселения IX–XII ст. на Дону и Тамани по археологическим памятникам.* Материалы и исследования по археологии СССР 6. 1941, 191–246.
Паршина 2001	Паршина, Е. А.: Клейменная византийская амфора X в. из Ласпи. In: *Морська торгівля в Північному Причорномор'ї.* Київ 2001, 104–117.
Паршина – Созник 2012	Паршина, Е. А. – Созник, В. В.: Амфорная тара Партенита (по материалам раскопок 1985–1988 гг.). In: *1000 років візантійської торгівлі (V–XV століття). Збірка наукових праць.* Бібліотека Vita Antiqua. Київ 2012, 7–42.
Паршина – Тесленко – Зеленко 2001	Паршина, Е. А. – Тесленко, И. Б. – Зеленко, С. М.: Гончарные центры Таврики VIII–X вв. In: *Морська торгівля в Північному Причорномор'ї.* Київ 2001, 52–81.

Плетнева 1959	Плетнева, С. А.: Керамика Саркела-Белой Вежи. In: *Труды Волго-Донской археологической экспедиции* II. Материалы и исследования по археологии СССР 75. Москва–Ленинград 1959, 212–272.
Плетнева 1963	Плетнева, С. А.: Средневековая керамика Таманского городища. In: *Керамика и стекло древней Тмутаракани.* Москва 1963, 5–72.
Плетнева 2006	Плетнева, С. А.: *Древнерусский город в кочевой степи: историко-стратиграфическое исследование.* Воронеж 2006.
Рамишвили 1965	Рамишвили, Р. М.: Археологические раскопки в Бичвинта (предварительный отчет раскопок 1958 г.). *Материалы по археологии Грузии и Кавказа* IV (1965) 107–122.
Рикман et al. 1971	Рикман, Э. А. – Рафалович, И. А. – Хынку, И. Г.: *Очерки истории культуры Молдавии: (II–XIV вв.).* Кишинев 1971.
Романчук 1976	Романчук, А. И.: *Херсонес VI – первой половины IX в.* Свердловск 1976.
Романчук 1983	Романчук, А. И.: Граффити на средневековых амфорах из портового района Херсонеса. *Античная древность и средние века* 20 (1983) 64–87.
Романчук – Сазанов – Седикова 1995	Романчук, А. И. – Сазанов, А. В. – Седикова, Л. В.: *Амфоры из комплексов византийского Херсона.* Екатеринбург 1995.
Сазанов 1989	Сазанов, А. В.: О хронологии Боспора ранневизантийского времени. *Советская Археология* 1989/4. 41–60.
Сорочан 2005	Сорочан, С. Б.: *Византийский Херсон (вторая пол. VI – первая пол. X вв.): Очерки истории и культуры.* Харьков 2005.

Чангова et al. 1981	Чангова, Й. – Радунчева, А. – Любенова, В. – Томова, В. – Юрукова, И.: *Перник I. Поселищен живот на хълма Кракра от V хил. пр. н. е. до VI в. н.е.* София 1981.
Чхаидзе 2008	Чхаидзе, В. Н.: *Таматарха. Раннесредневековый город на Таманском полуострове.* Москва 2008.
Якобсон 1950	Якобсон, А. Л.: *Средневековый Херсонес (XII–XIV вв.).* Материалы и исследования по археологии СССР 17. Москва–Ленинград 1950.
Якобсон 1951	Якобсон, А. Л.: Средневековы амфор Северног Причерноморья. *Советская Археология* 15 (1951) 325–344.
Якобсон 1970	Якобсон, А. Л.: *Раннесредневековые сельские поселения юго-западной Таврики.* Ленинград 1970.
Якобсон 1979	Якобсон, А. Л.: *Керамика и керамическое производство средневековой Таврики.* Ленинград 1979.

Maps

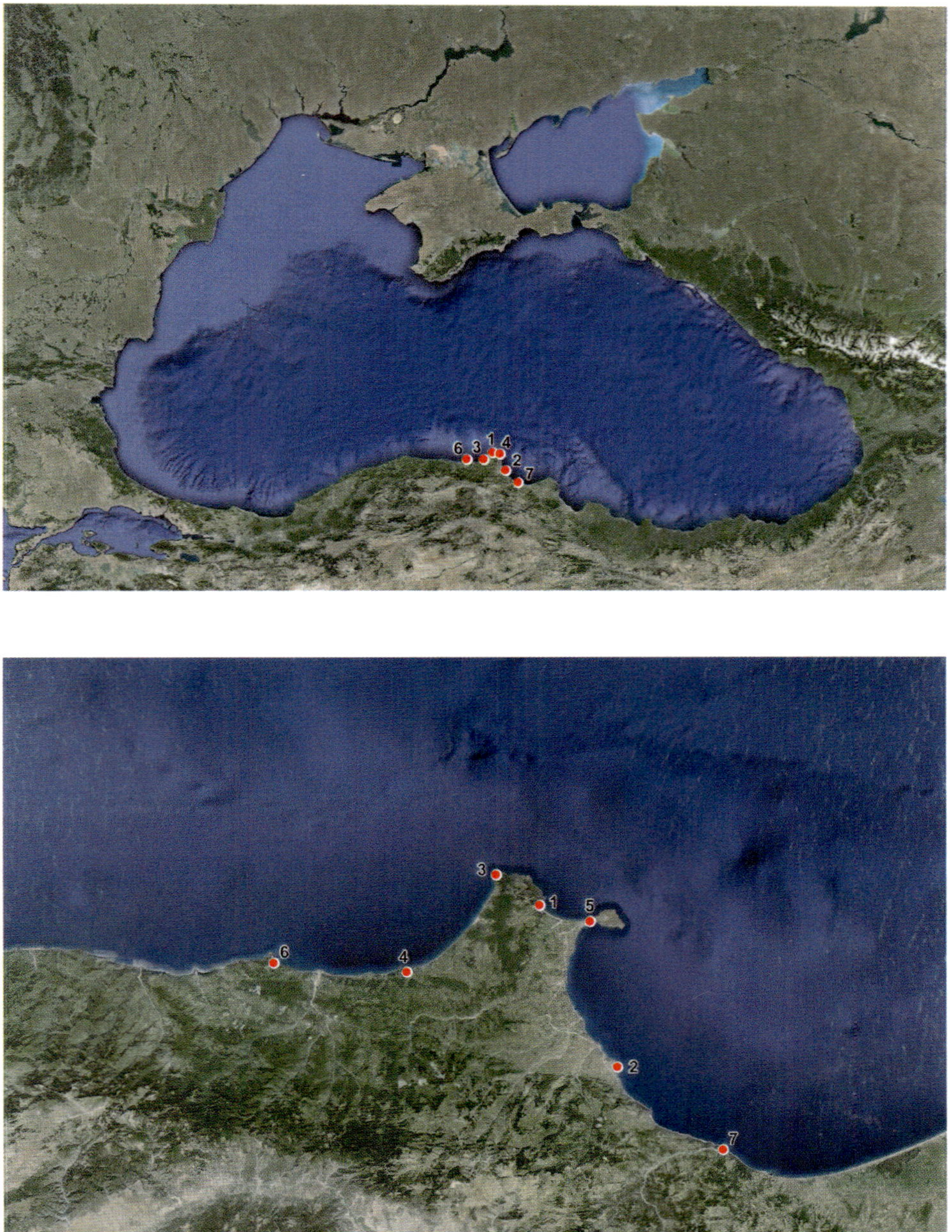

Map 1. Harbours around Sinope in late antiquity and the early Middle Ages: 1. Harmene (Akliman), 2. Karousa (Gerze), 3. Lepte Akra (İnceburun), 4. Potamoi (near Ayancık), 5. Sinope (Sinop) 6. Stephane (Caylıoğlu near Ayancık), 7. Zagora (Çayağzı)

Map 2. Distribution of early medieval (Crimean) amphorae: 1. Chaban-Kule, 2. Kanakskaia Balka, 3. Karantinnaia bukhta, 4. Kerch, 5. Kherson, 6. Radiogorka, 7. Sarkel, 8. Sinop, 9. Tmutarakan/Tamatarkha

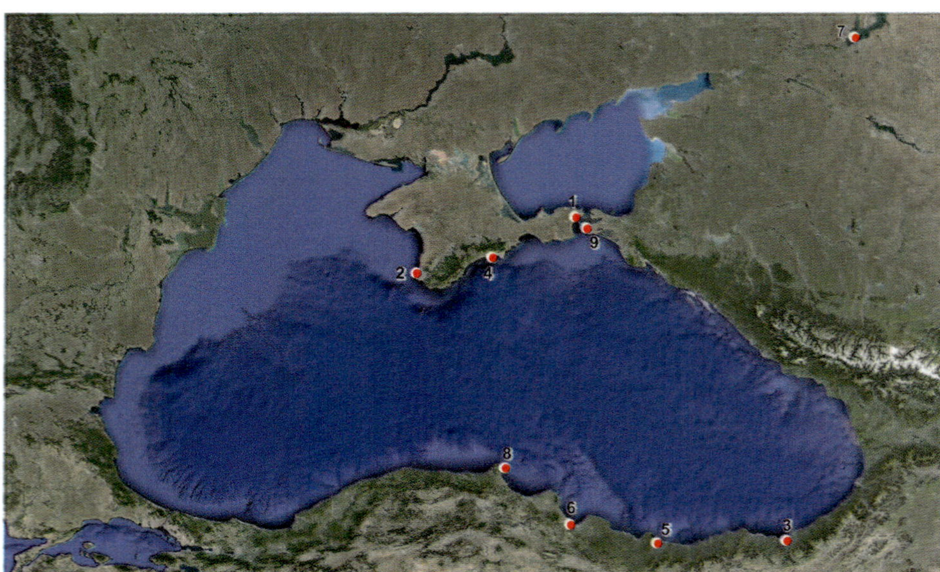

Map 3. Distribution of Tmutarakan jugs: 1. Kerch, 2. Kherson, 3. Kuşlucaköy (Çamburnu, Trabzon), Novy Svet, 4. Ordu, 6. Samsun, 7. Sarkel, 8. Sinop, 9. Tmutarakan/Tamatarkha

Plates

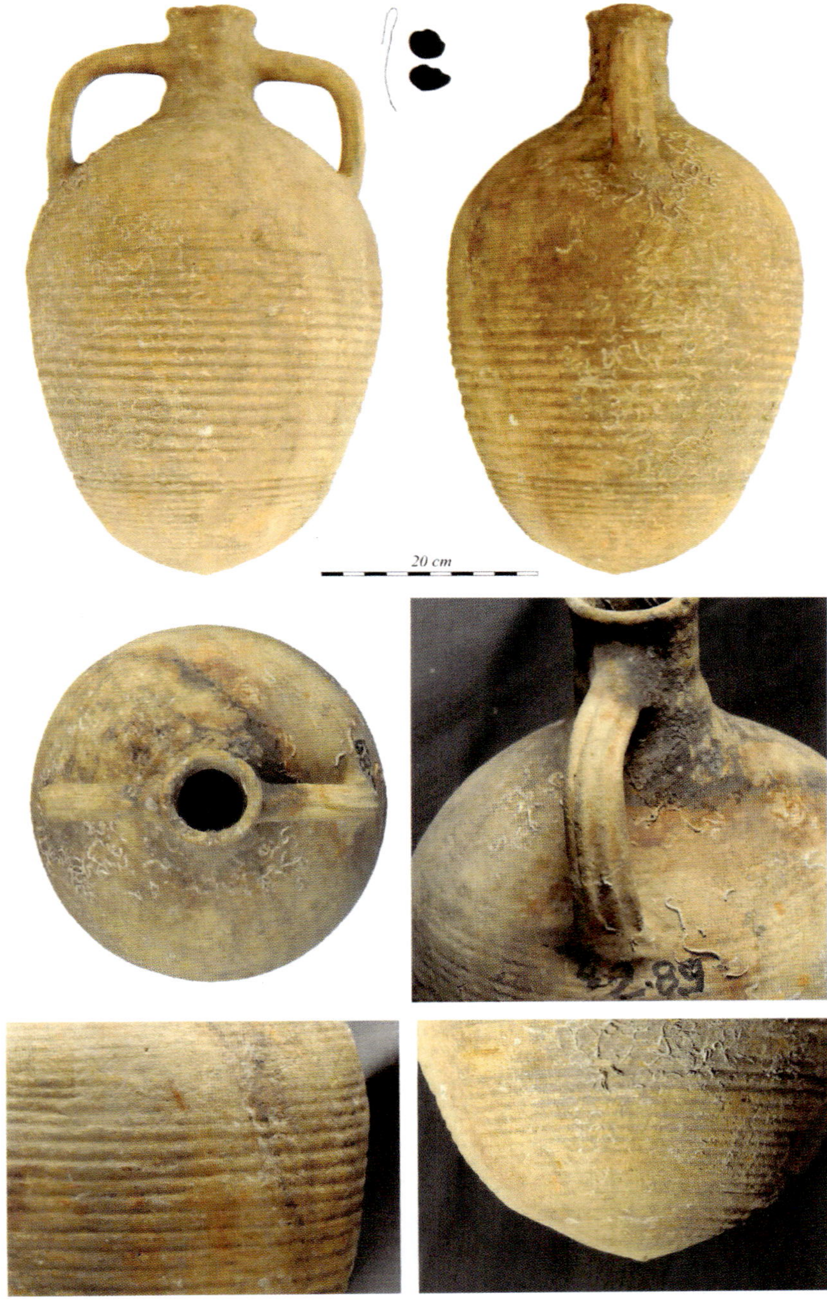

Plate 1. LR 1A type amphora from the Black Sea, probably found at Ayancık (Cat. no. 1)

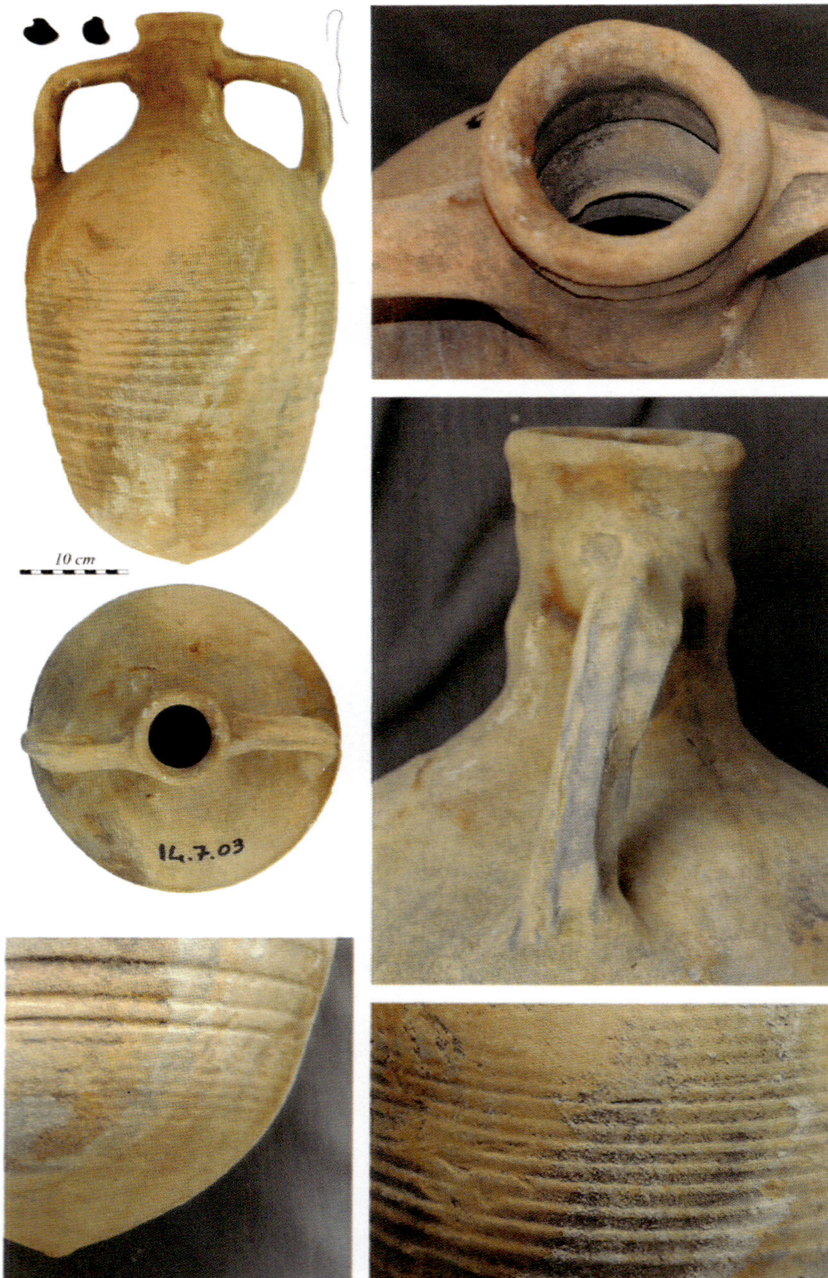

Plate 2. LR 1A type amphora from the Black Sea, from a US underwater survey (Cat. no. 2)

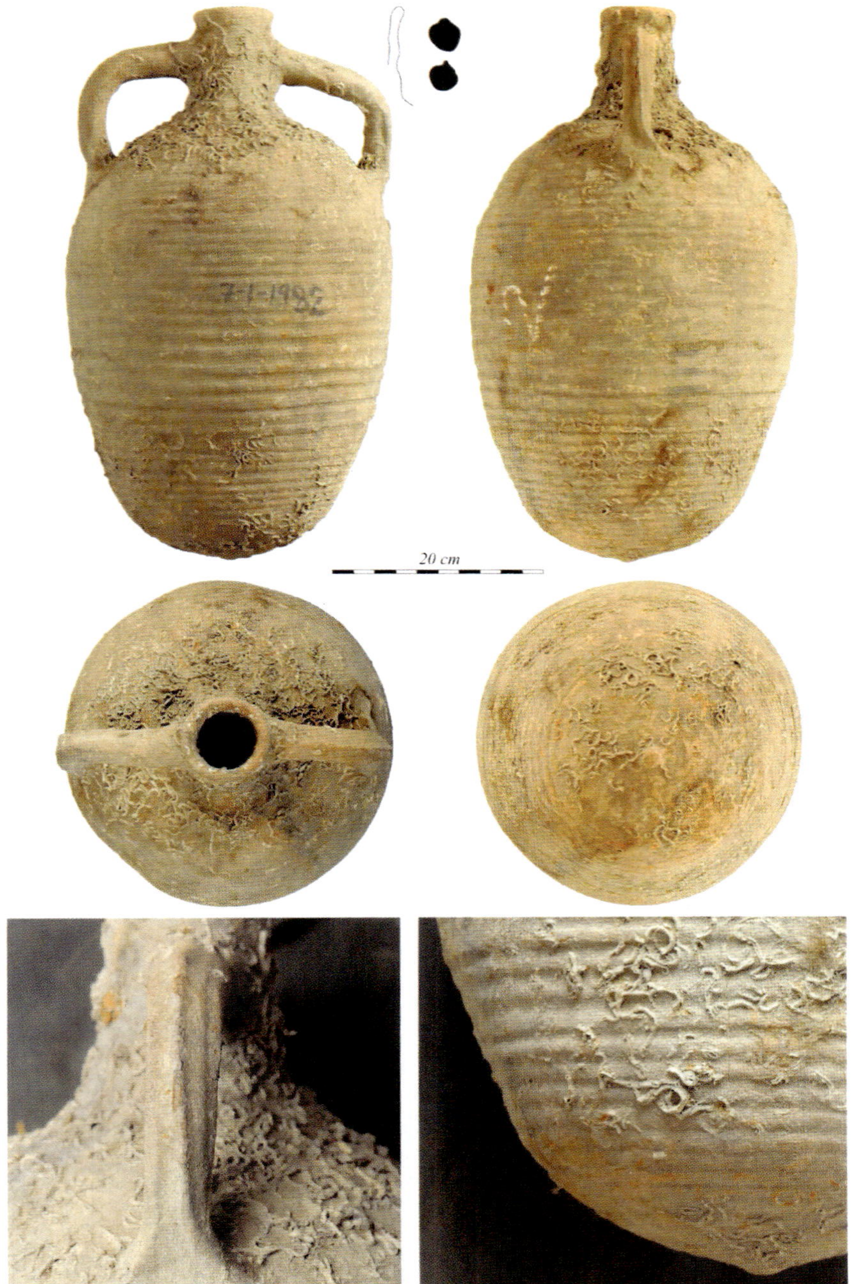

Plate 3. LR 1A type amphora from the Black Sea found by fisherman Recep Batman probably near Sinop (Cat. no. 3)

Plate 4. LR 1A type amphora from the Black Sea found by Mustafa Kaymak, resident of Sinop (Cat. no. 4)

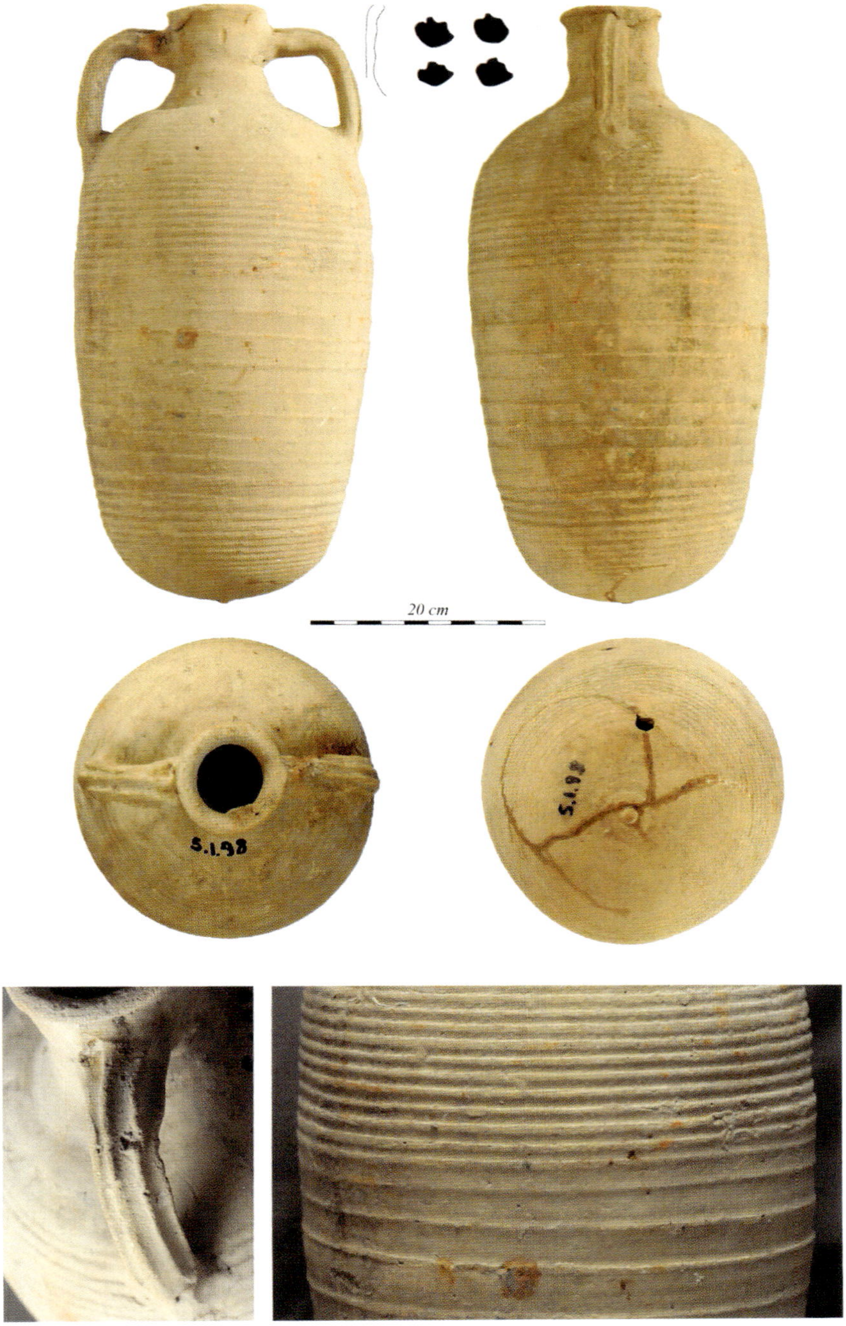

Plate 5. LR 1B type amphora from the Black Sea found by Alsen Gerginci, resident of Sinop (Cat. no. 5)

Plate 6. LR 1B type amphora from the Black Sea at Yakakent, found by fisherman İlyas Gün (Cat. no. 6)

Plate 7. LR 1B type amphora from the Black Sea, donated by Mustafa Kemal Koca (Cat. no. 7)

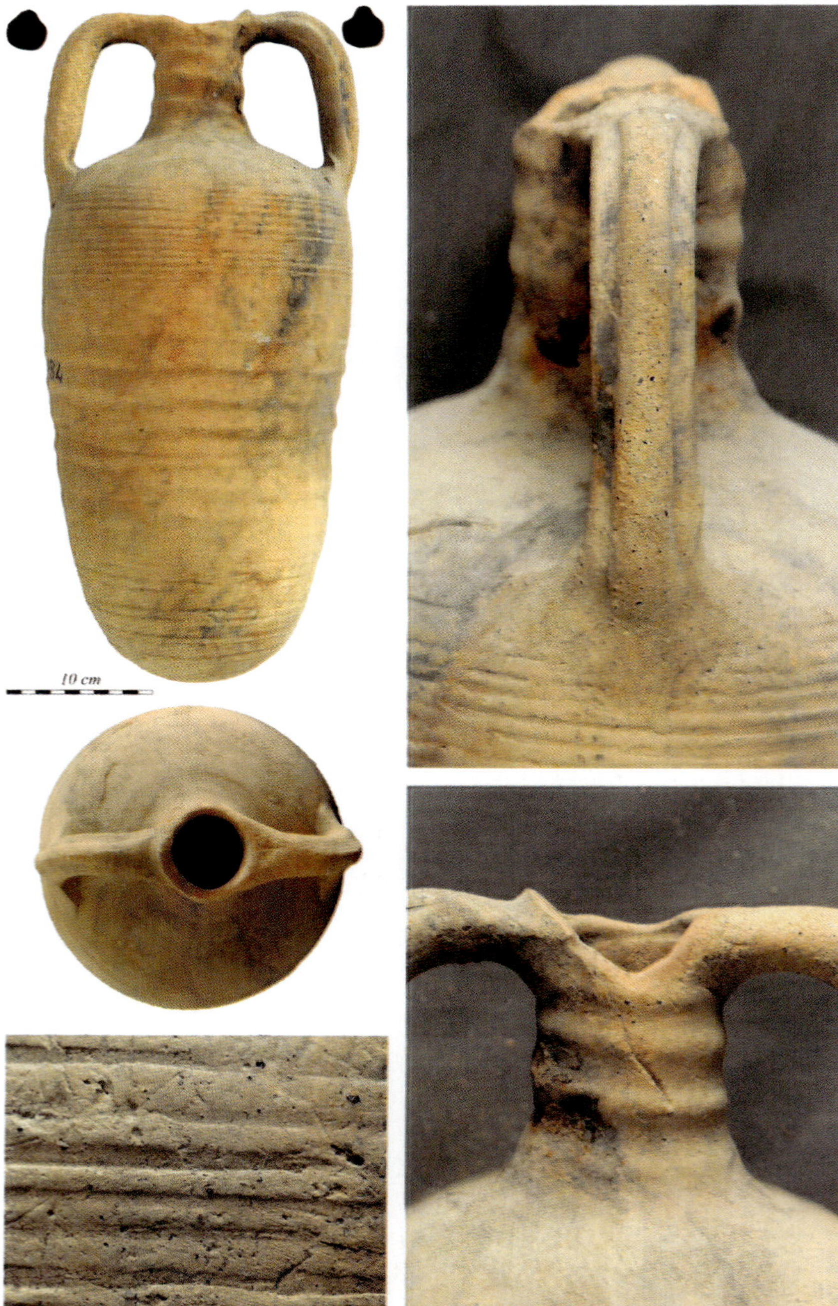

Plate 8. LR 1B type amphora, probably from the Black Sea (Cat. no. 8)

Plate 9. LR 1B type amphora from the Black Sea, donation from the Turkish Coast Guard (Cat. no. 9)

Plate 10. LR 1B type amphora, probably from the Black Sea, purchased from Şükrü Özdemir, resident of Ayancık (Cat. no. 10)

Plate 11. LR 2 type amphora from the Black Sea, purchased from Şükrü Özdemir, resident of Ayancık (Cat. no. 11)

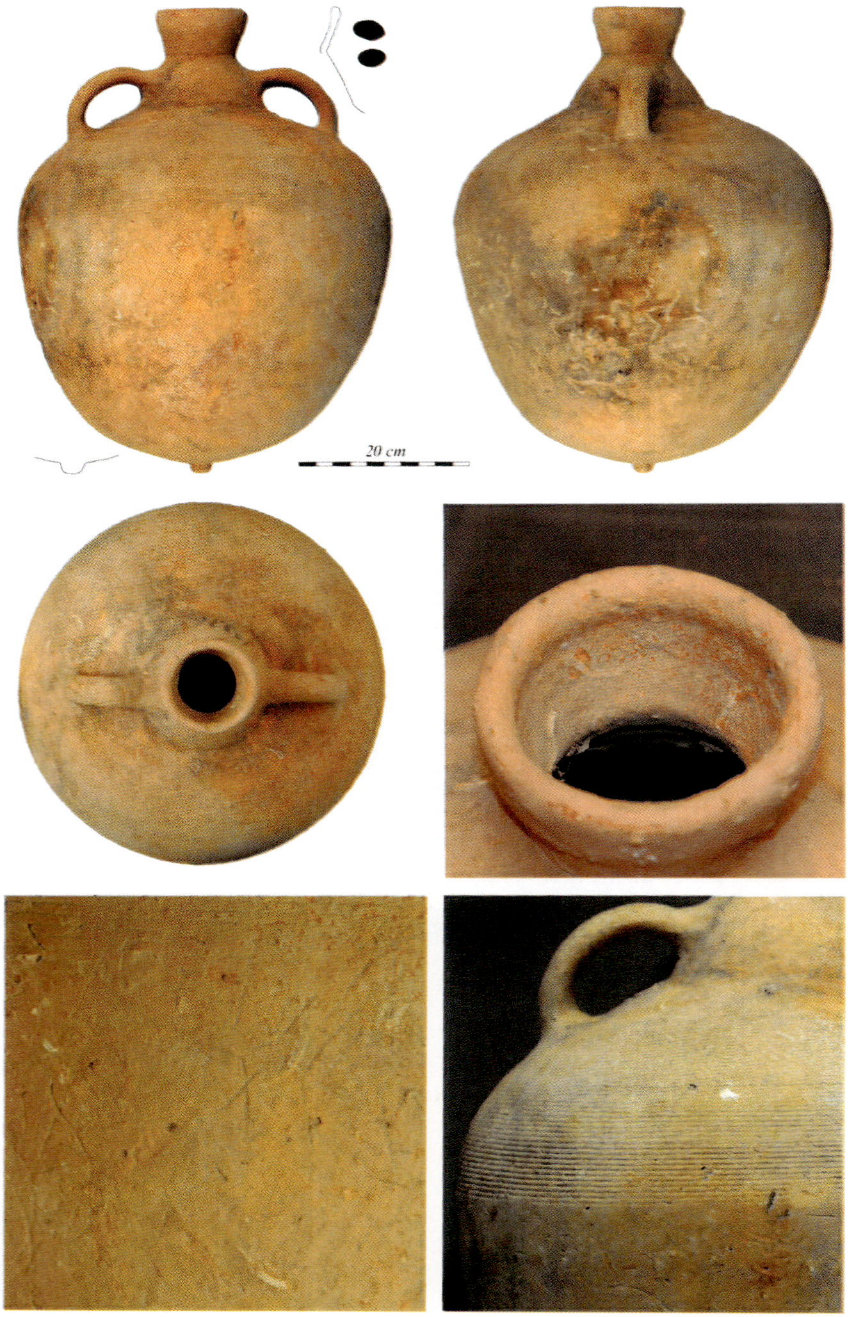

Plate 12. LR 2 type amphora from the Black Sea, purchased from Dr. İbrahim Önder, resident of Sinop (Cat. no. 12)

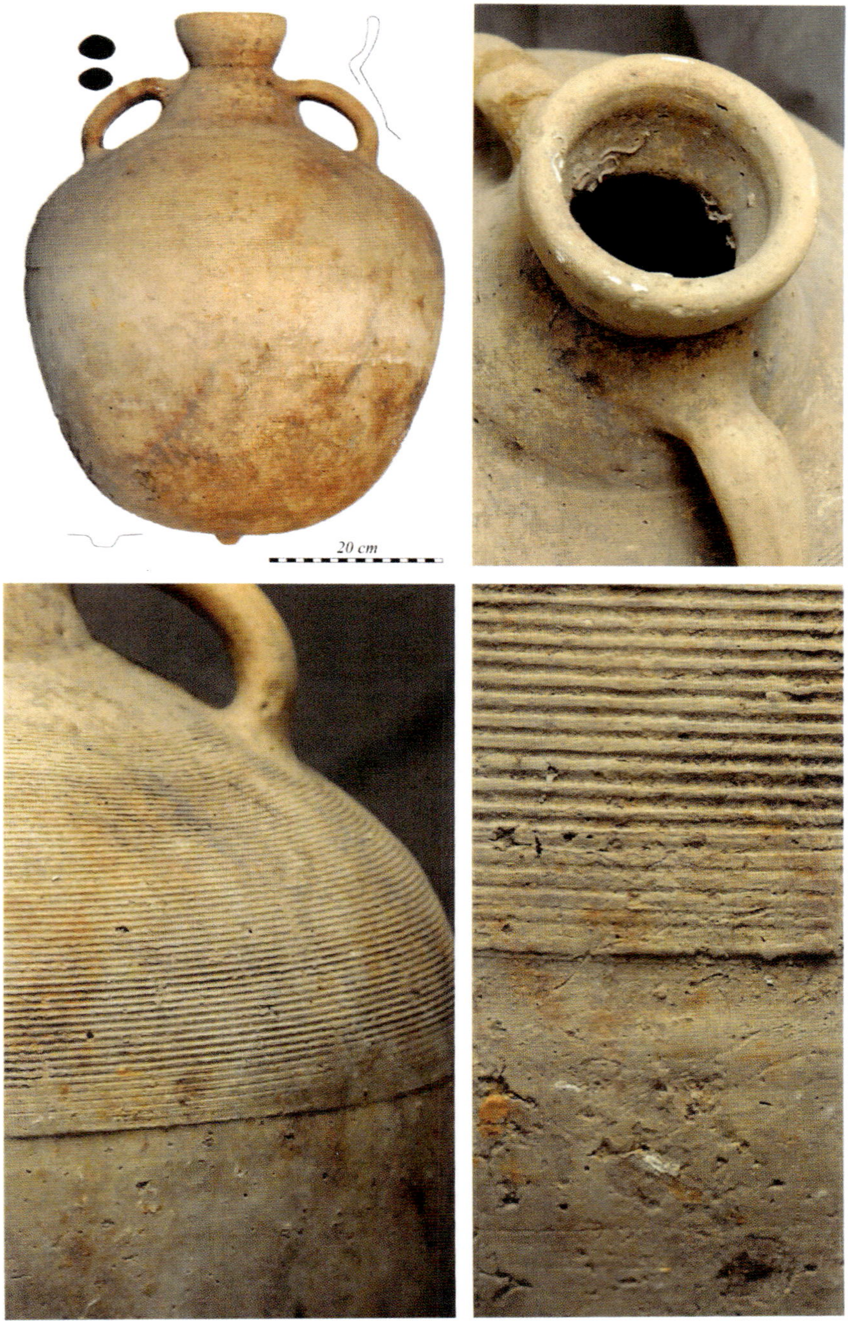

Plate 13. LR 2 type amphora from the Black Sea, purchased from Dr. İbrahim Önder, resident of Sinop (Cat. no. 13)

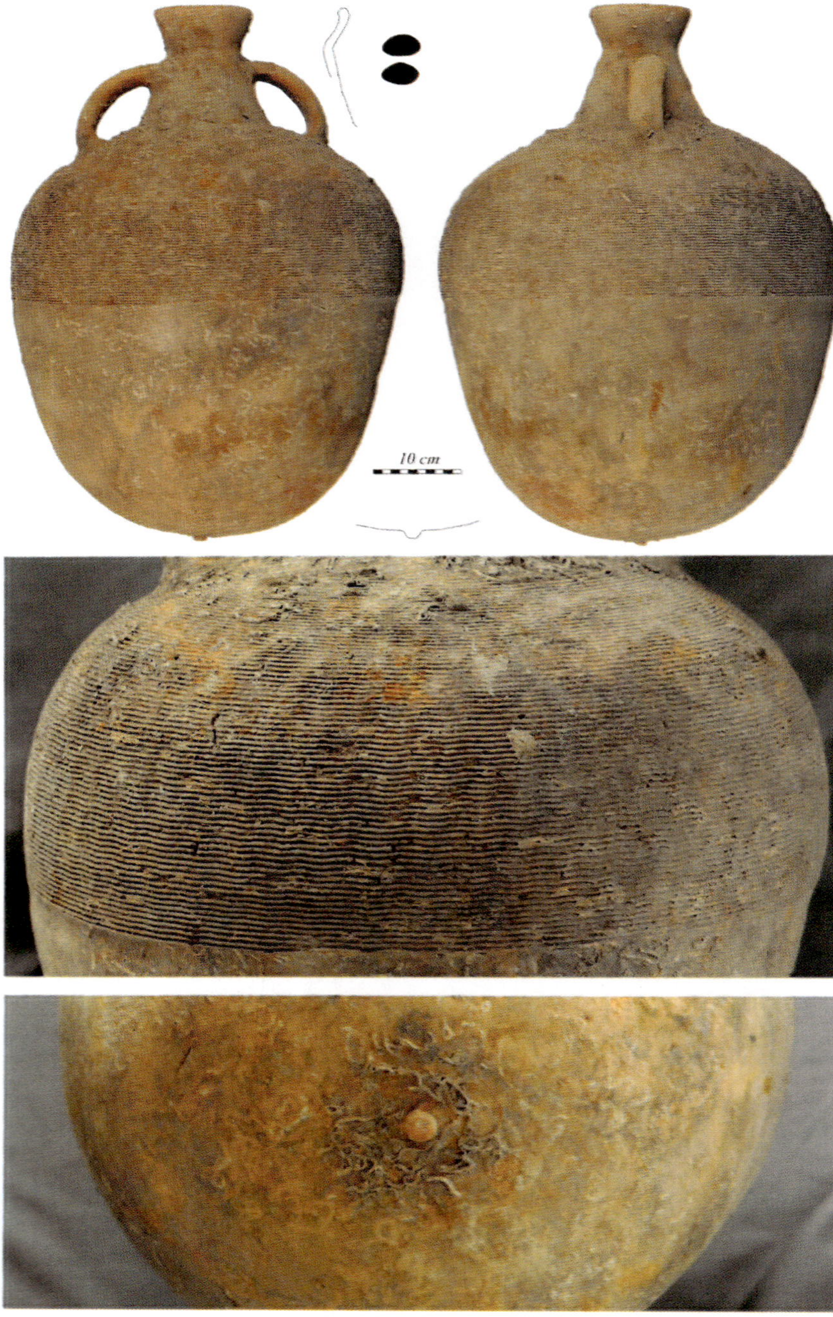

Plate 14. LR 2 type amphora from the Black Sea, purchased from Nihat Kayas (Cat. no. 14)

Plate 15. LR 2C type amphora from the Black Sea, purchased from Şükrü Gümüş, resident of Sinop (Cat. no. 15)

Plate 16. LR 2C type amphora from the Black Sea, purchased from Durmuş Semiz (Cat. no. 16)

Plate 17. LR 2C type amphora from the Black Sea, purchased from fisherman Ömer Saral (Cat. no. 17)

Plate 18. LR 2C type amphora from the Black Sea, purchased from fisherman Mustafa Arslan (Cat. no. 18)

Plate 19. LR 2C type amphora from the Black Sea, purchased from fisherman Mustafa Arslan (Cat. no. 19)

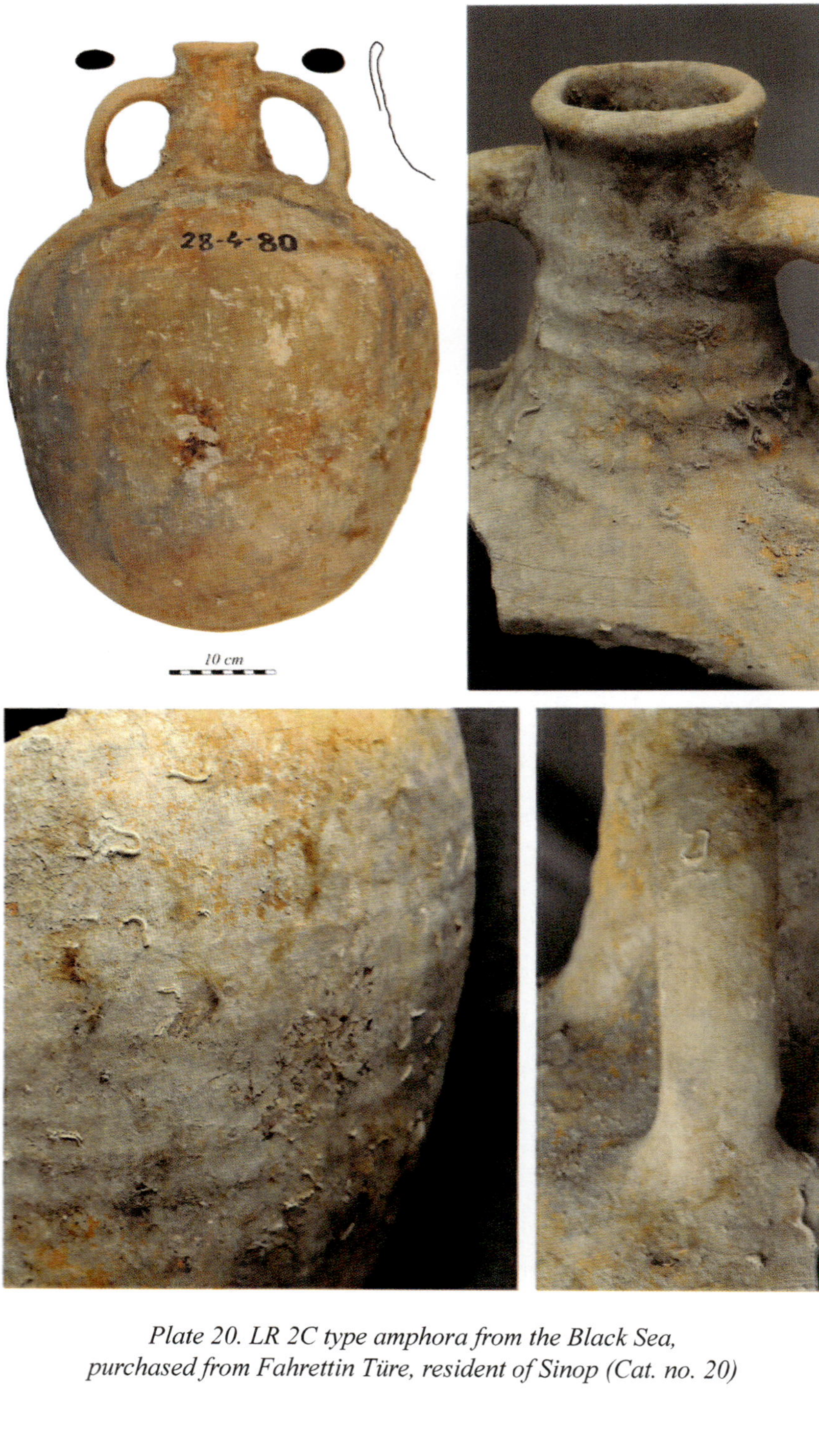

Plate 20. LR 2C type amphora from the Black Sea, purchased from Fahrettin Türe, resident of Sinop (Cat. no. 20)

Plate 21. LR 2C type amphora from the Black Sea, purchased from İbrahim Önder, resident of Sinop (Cat. no. 21)

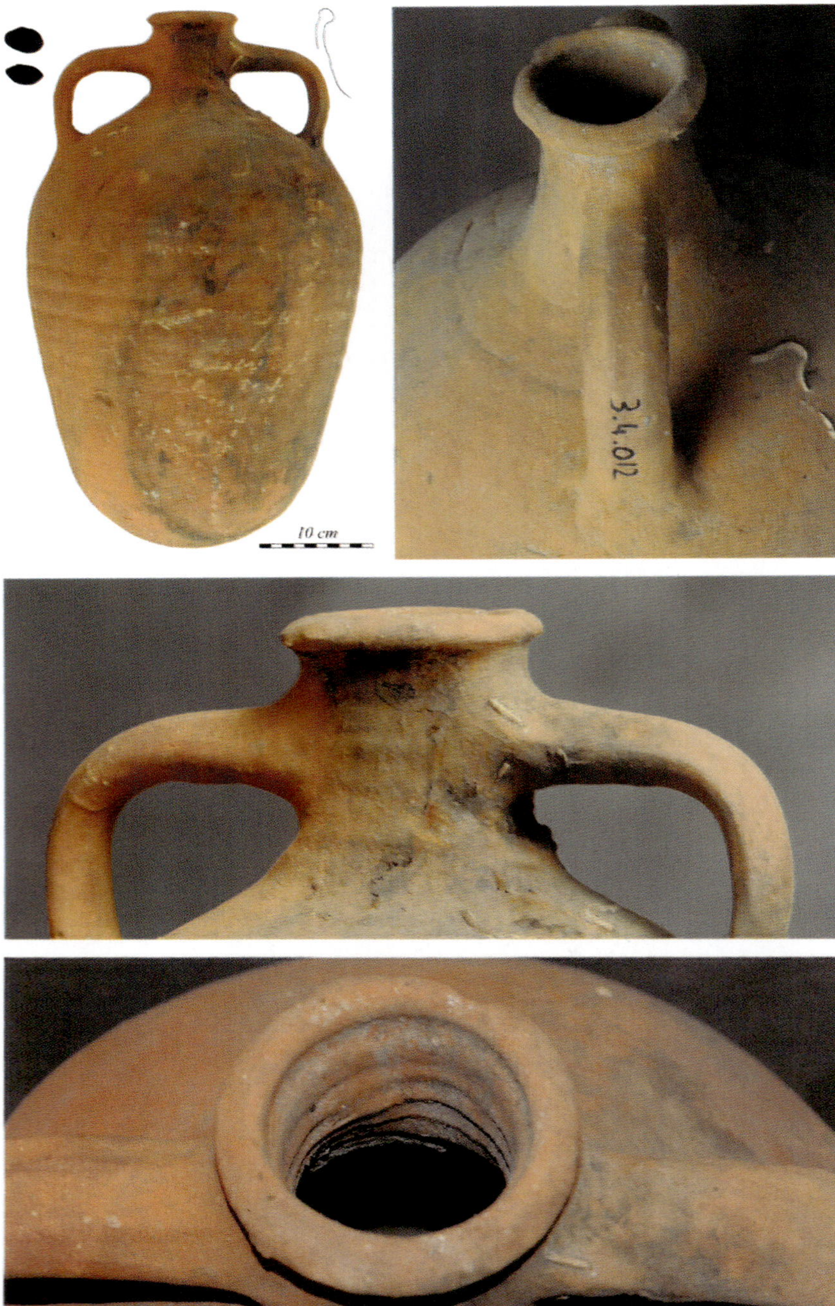

Plate 22. Crimean amphora of variant 1 from the Black Sea at Ayancık, purchased from Şükrü Özdemir (Cat. no. 22)

Plate 23. Crimean amphora of variant 1 from the Black Sea at the village of Kuşluca, Trabzon, purchased from Ali Arslan (Cat. no. 23)

Plate 24. Crimean amphora of variant 1 from the Black Sea, found by the marine department of the police headquarters (Cat. no. 24)

Plate 25. Crimean amphora of variant 1 from the Black Sea, purchased from Saim Arslan (Cat. no. 25)

Plate 26. Crimean amphora of variant 2 from the Black Sea at the village of Kuşluca, Trabzon, purchased from Ali Arslan (Cat. no. 26)

Plate 27. Crimean amphora of variant 2 from the Black Sea, purchased from fisherman Şükrü Gümüş, resident of Sinop (Cat. no. 27)

Plate 28. Crimean amphora of variant 2 from the Black Sea, purchased from fisherman Mustafa Kaymak, resident of Sinop (Cat. no. 28)

Plate 29. Crimean amphora of variant 2 from the Black Sea, purchased from Tayfun Güner, resident of Sinop (Cat. no. 29)

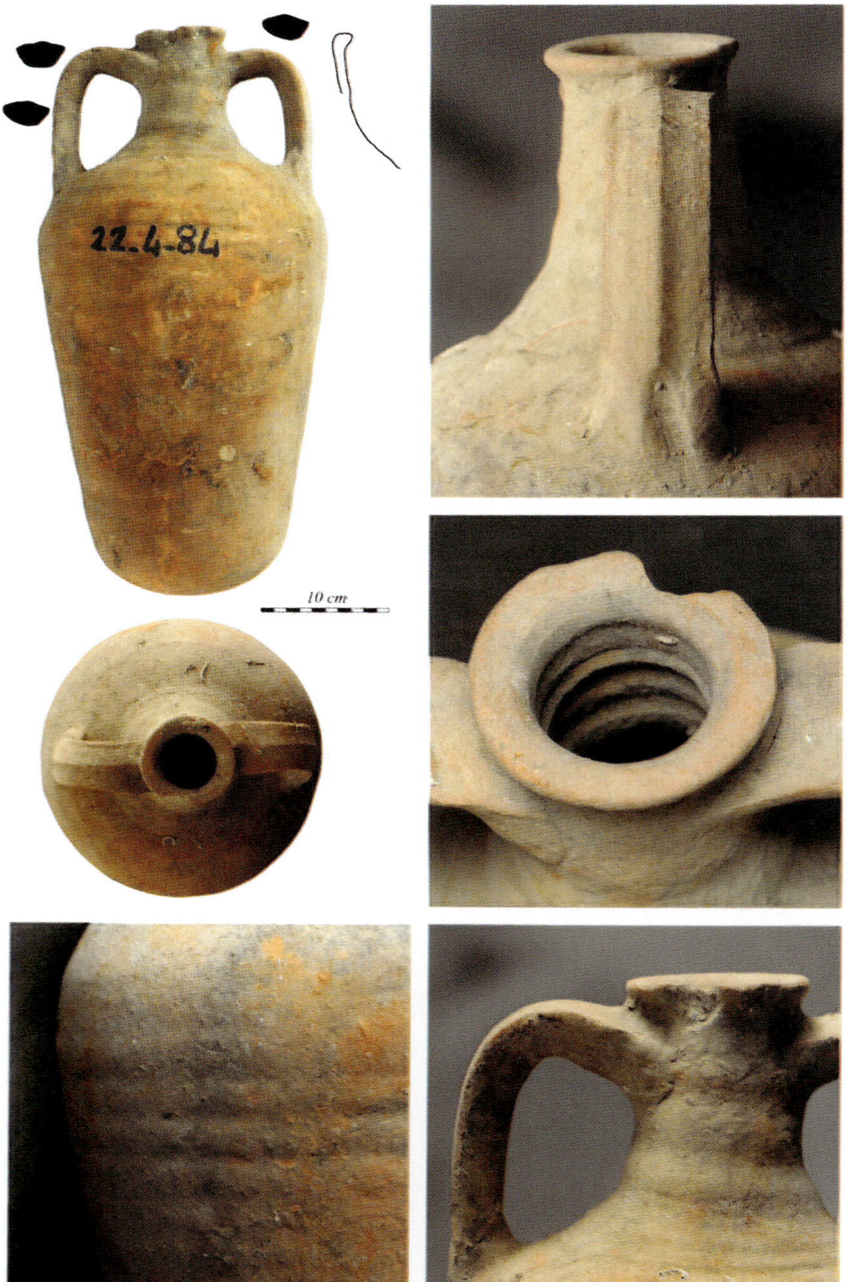

Plate 30. Crimean amphora of variant 2 from the Black Sea, purchased from Nurettin Zarflıoğlu (Cat. no. 30)

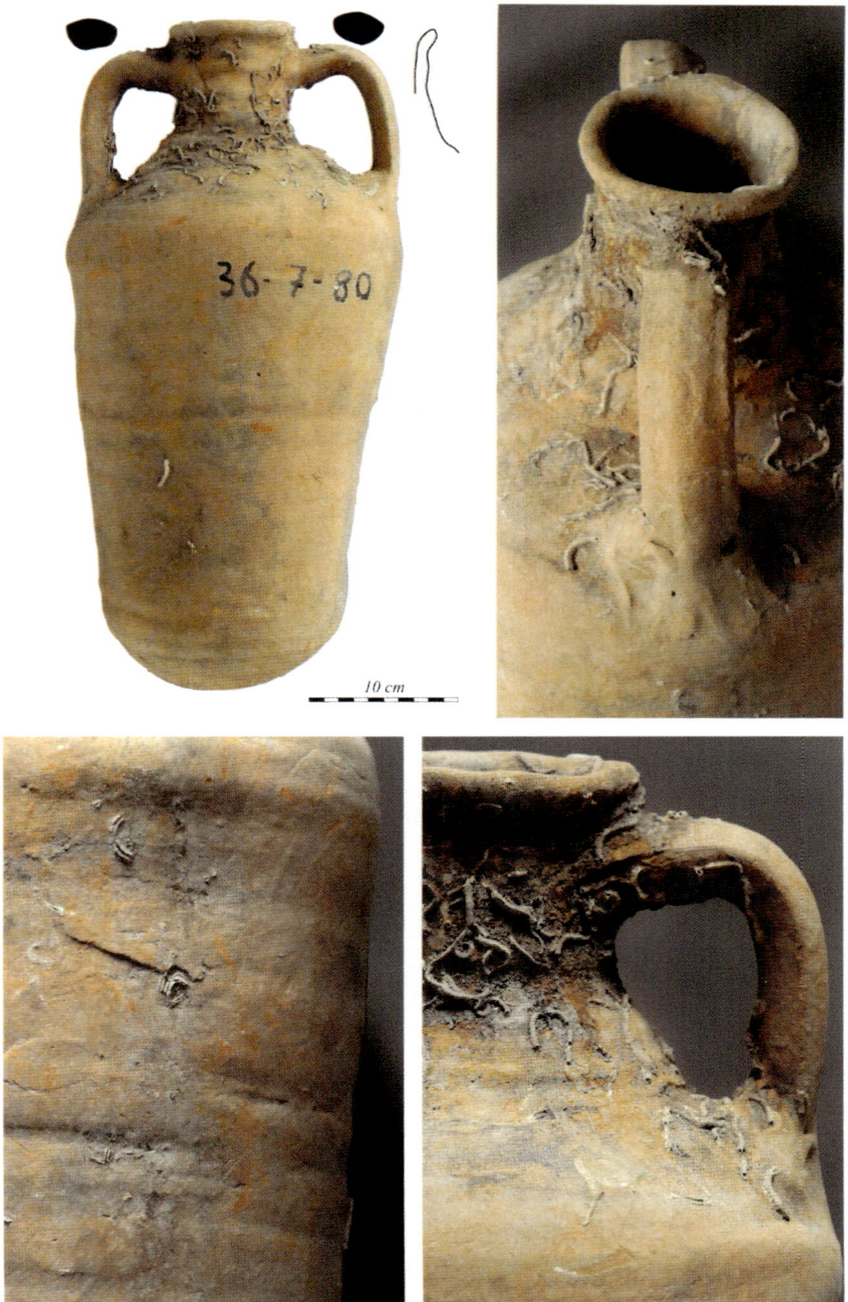

Plate 31. Crimean amphora of variant 2 from the Black Sea, purchased from Mustafa Arslan (Cat. no. 31)

Plate 32. Crimean amphora of variant 2 from the shipwreck found near Karakum, donated by the High School for Water Management (Cat. no. 32)

Plate 33. Tall-necked Günsenin 1 amphora from the Black Sea at Ayancık, purchased from Şükrü Özdemir (Cat. no. 33)

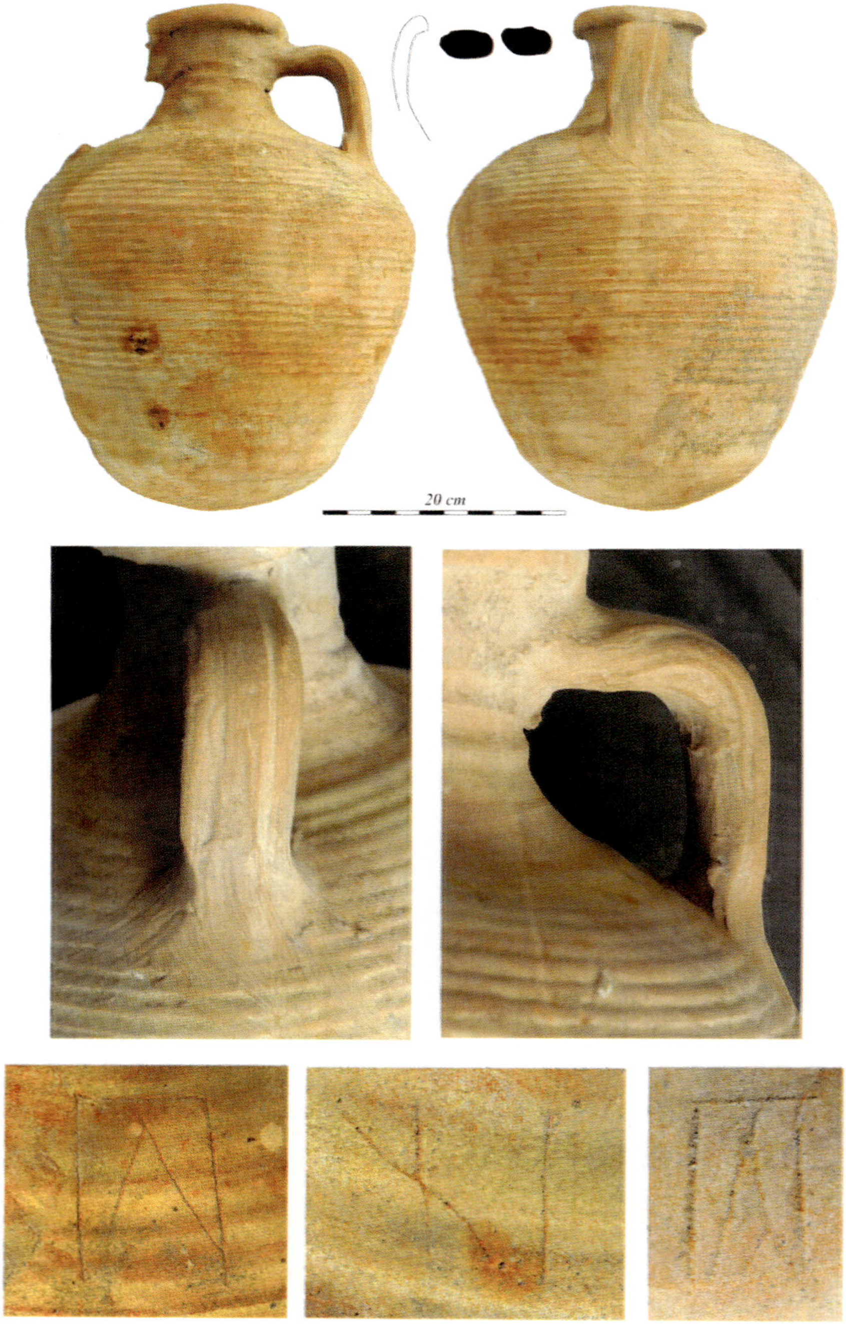

Plate 34. Tall-necked Günsenin 1 amphora from the Black Sea, purchased from fisherman Şükrü Gümüş, resident of Sinop (Cat. no. 34)

Plate 35. Tall-necked Günsenin 1 amphora from the Black Sea at the village of Kuşluca, Trabzon, purchased from Ali Arslan (Cat. no. 35)

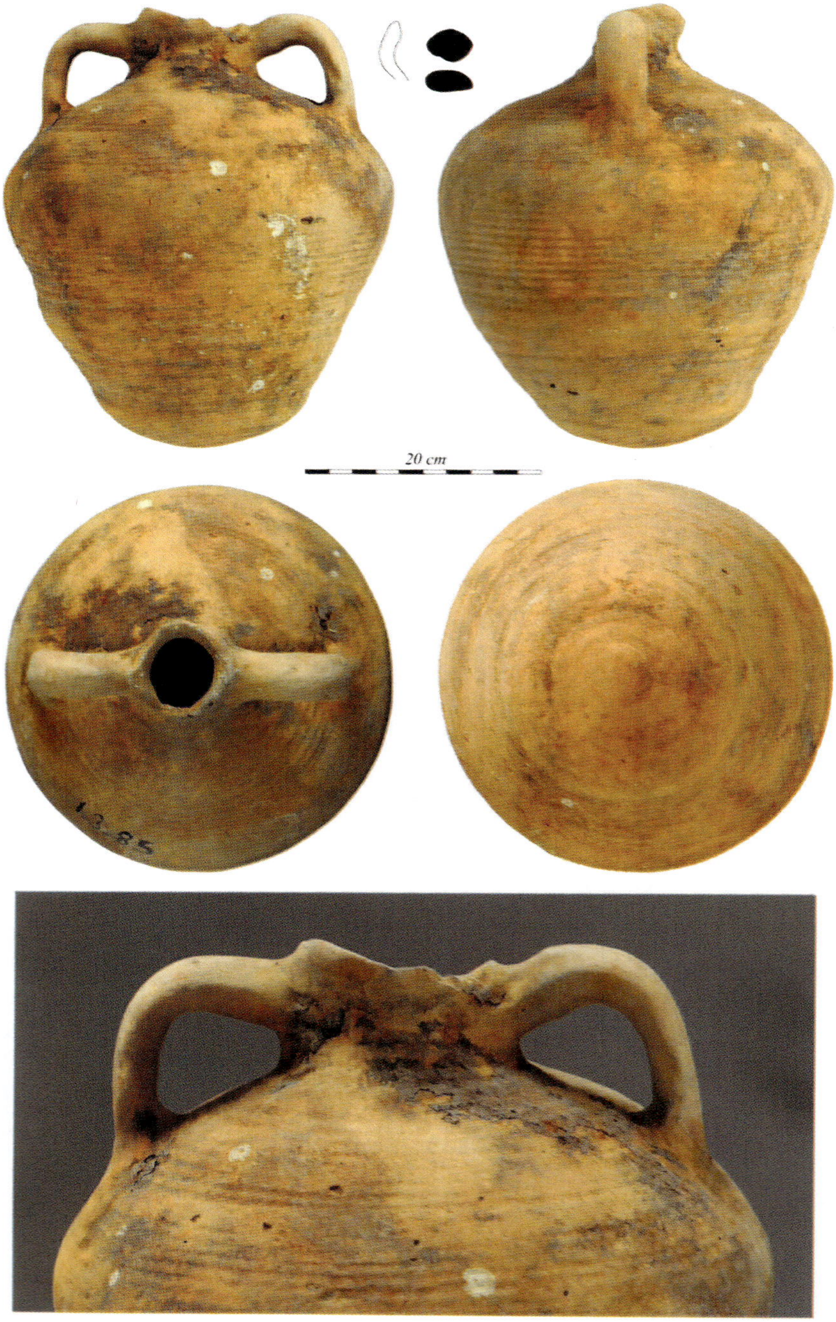

Plate 36. Günsenin 1 amphora from the Black Sea, purchased from Erdal Batmaz, resident of Sinop (Cat. no. 36)

Plate 37. Günsenin 1 amphora from the Black Sea,
purchased from fisherman Şükrü Gümüş, resident of Sinop (Cat. no. 37)

Plate 38. Günsenin 1 amphora from the Black Sea, donated by the Coast Guard (Cat. no. 38)

*Plate 39. Günsenin 1 amphora from the Black Sea,
purchased from Mustafa Arslan, resident of Sinop (Cat. no. 39)*

Plate 40. Günsenin 1 amphora from the Black Sea,
purchased from Mustafa Arslan, resident of Sinop (Cat. no. 40)

Plate 41. Günsenin 1 amphora from the Black Sea,
purchased from fisherman Tayfun Güner, resident of Sinop (Cat. no. 41)

*Plate 42. Günsenin 1 amphora from the Black Sea,
donated by fisherman Rifat Reis, resident of Sinop (Cat. no. 42)*

Plate 43. Günsenin 1 amphora from the Black Sea, from the area of the inner harbour at Sinop (Cat. no. 43)

Plate 44. Günsenin 1 amphora from the museum's old collection, originally housed in the Pervane madrasah (Cat. no. 44)

*Plate 45. Günsenin 1 amphora from the Black Sea,
purchased from fisherman Mustafa Arslan, resident of Sinop (Cat. no. 45)*

Plate 46. Günsenin 1 amphora from the Black Sea, purchased from fisherman Şükrü Gümüş, resident of Sinop (Cat. no. 46)

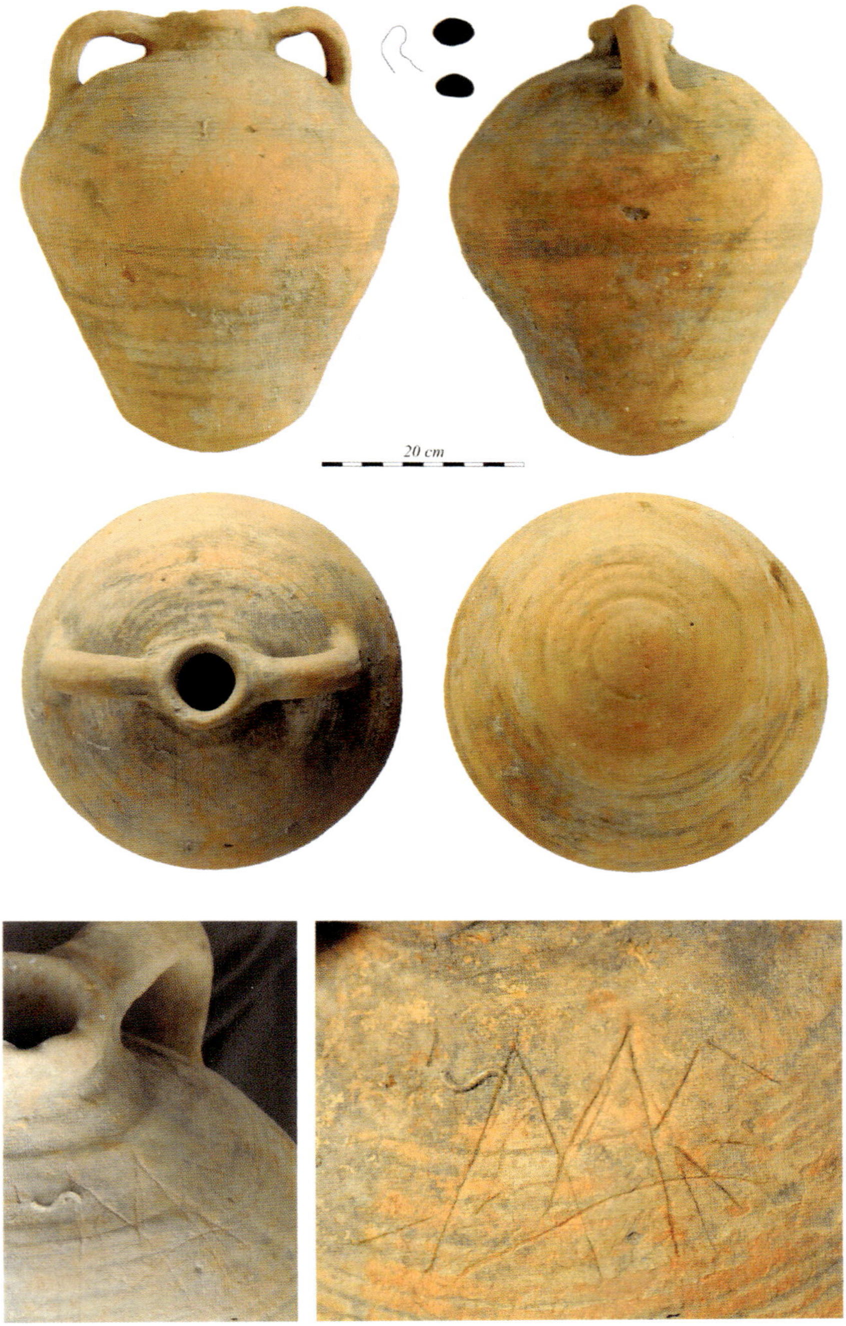

*Plate 47. Günsenin 1 amphora from the Black Sea,
purchased from fisherman Şükrü Gümüş, resident of Sinop (Cat. no. 47)*

Plate 48. Günsenin 1 amphora from the Black Sea,
purchased from Aysun Gezginci, resident of Sinop (Cat. no. 48)

Plate 49. Günsenin 1 amphora, purchased from Sayin Arslan, resident of Istanbul, Sarıyer (Cat. no. 49)

*Plate 50. Günsenin 1 amphora from the Black Sea,
purchased from Necati Çor, resident of Sinop (Cat. no. 50)*

Plate 51. Tmutarakan jug from the Black Sea,
purchased from fisherman Şükrü Gümüş, resident of Sinop (Cat. no. 51)

Plate 52. Tmutarakan jug from the Black Sea, purchased from fisherman Ali Arslan, resident of Kuşlucaköy, Trabzon (Cat. no. 52)

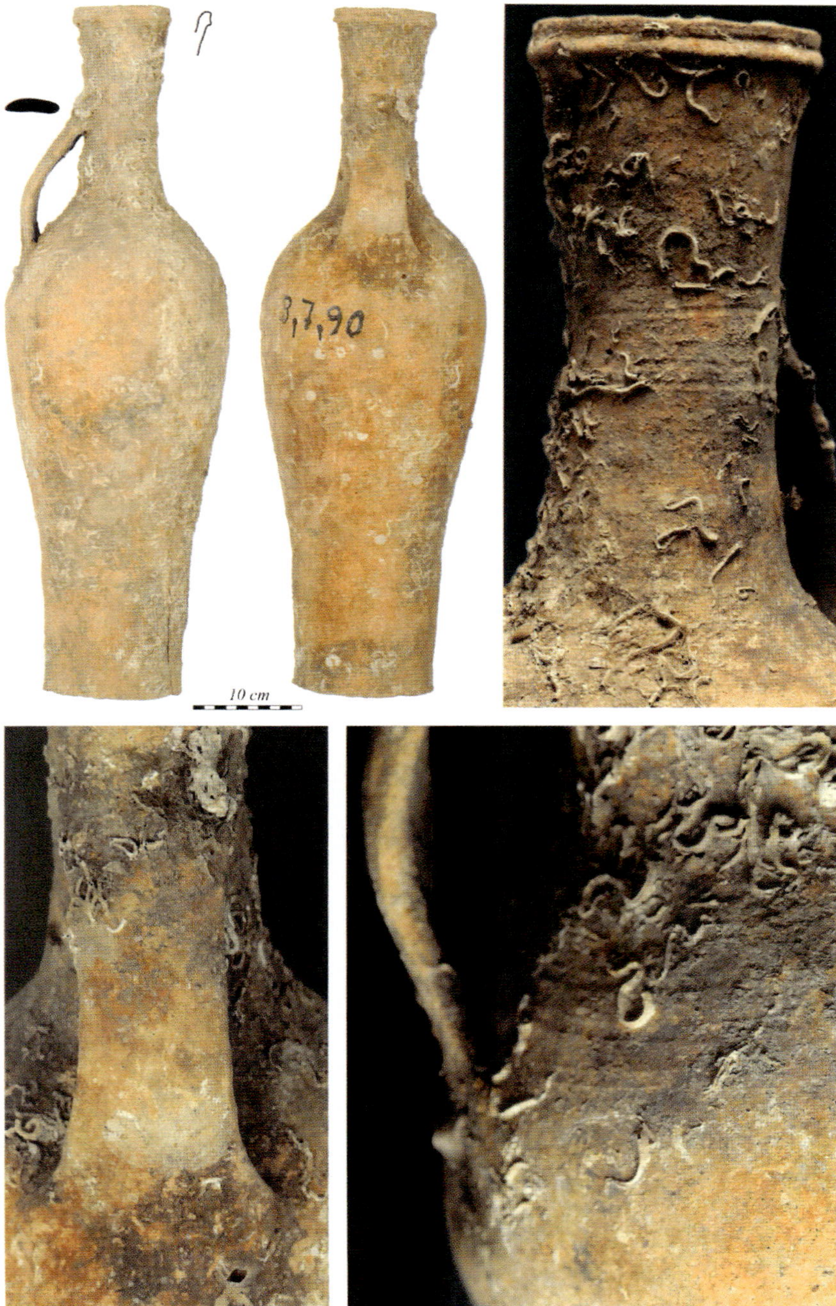

*Plate 53. Tmutarakan jug from the Black Sea,
purchased from fisherman Şükrü Gümüş, resident of Sinop (Cat. no. 53)*

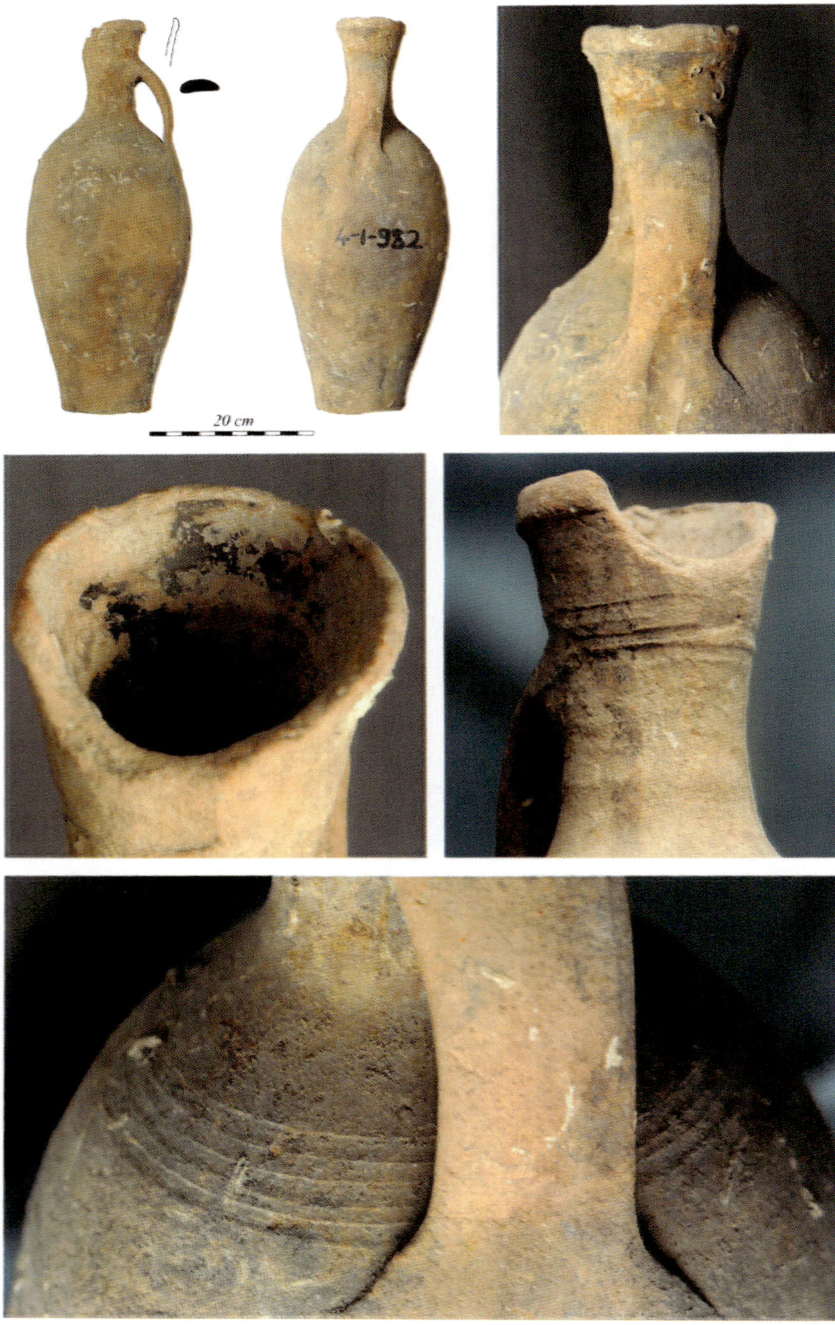

Plate 54. Tmutarakan jug from the Black Sea, purchased from fisherman Ali Arslan, resident of Kuşlucaköy, Trabzon (Cat. no. 54)

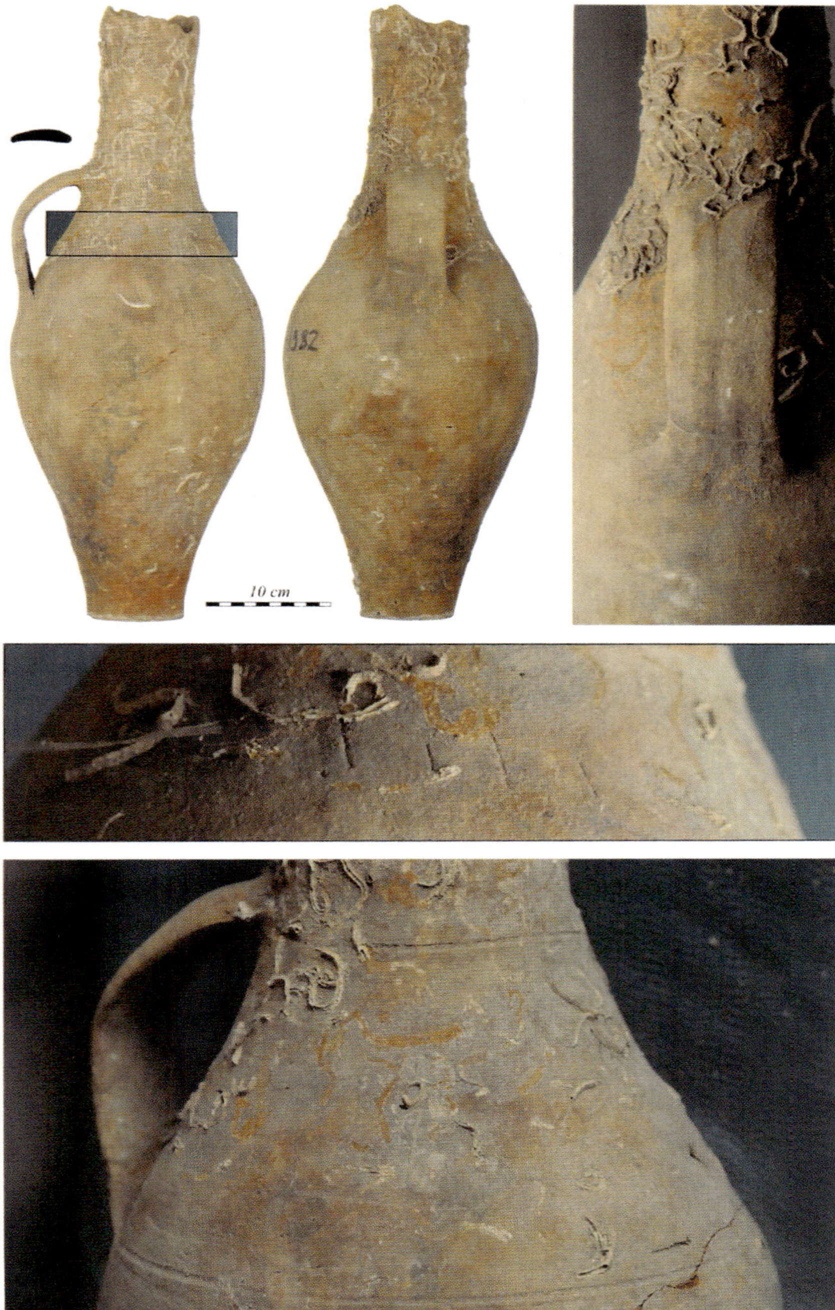

Plate 55. Tmutarakan jug from the Black Sea,
purchased from fisherman Ali Arslan, resident of Kuşlucaköy, Trabzon (Cat. no. 55)

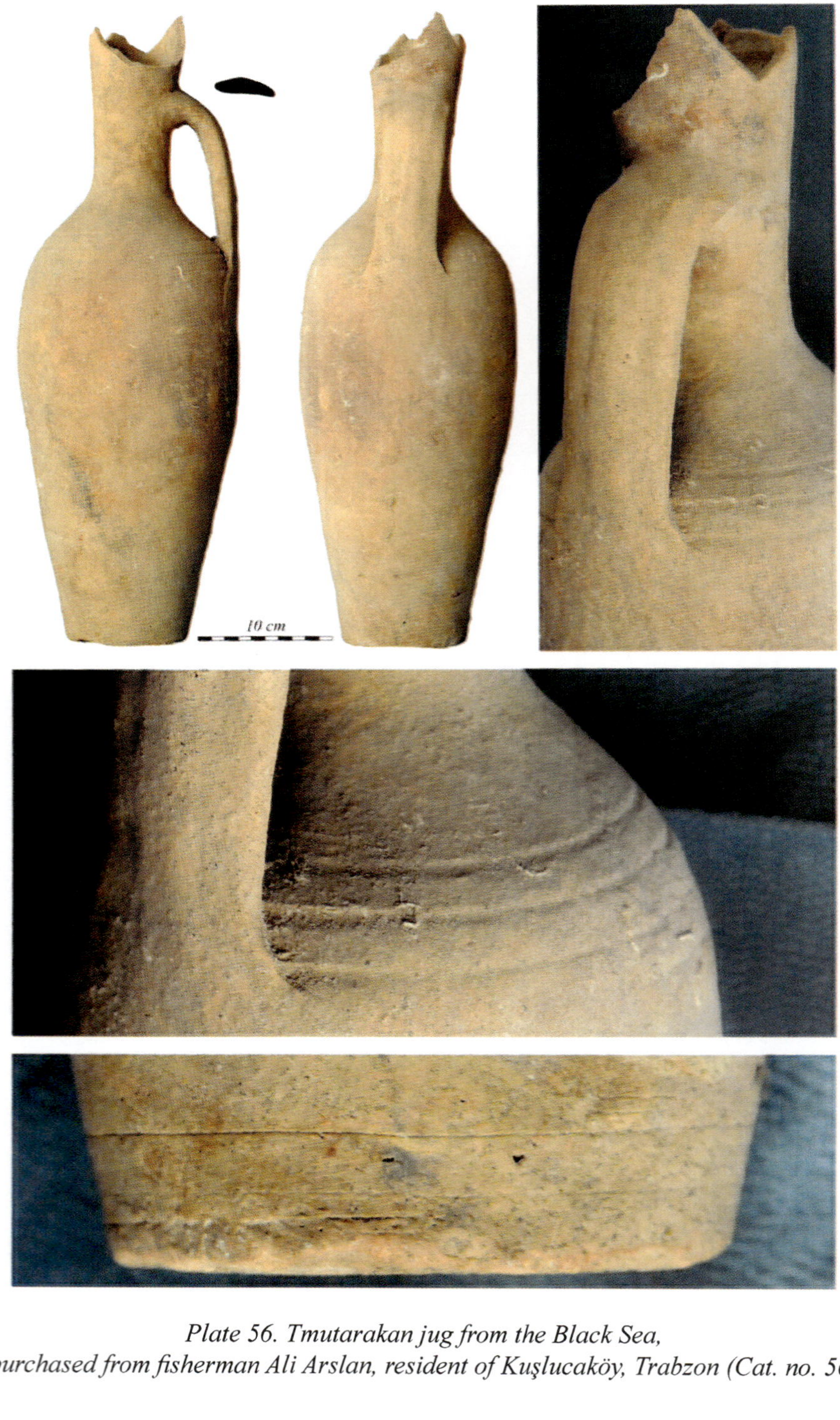

Plate 56. Tmutarakan jug from the Black Sea,
purchased from fisherman Ali Arslan, resident of Kuşlucaköy, Trabzon (Cat. no. 56)

Plate 57. Tmutarakan jug from the Black Sea,
purchased from fisherman Ali Arslan, resident of Kuşlucaköy, Trabzon (Cat. no. 57)

Plate 58. Tmutarakan jug from the Black Sea, purchased from Durmuş Semir, resident of Sinop (Cat. no. 58)

Plate 59. Tmutarakan jug from the Black Sea,
purchased from fisherman Kadır Kılıç, resident of Sinop (Cat. no. 59)

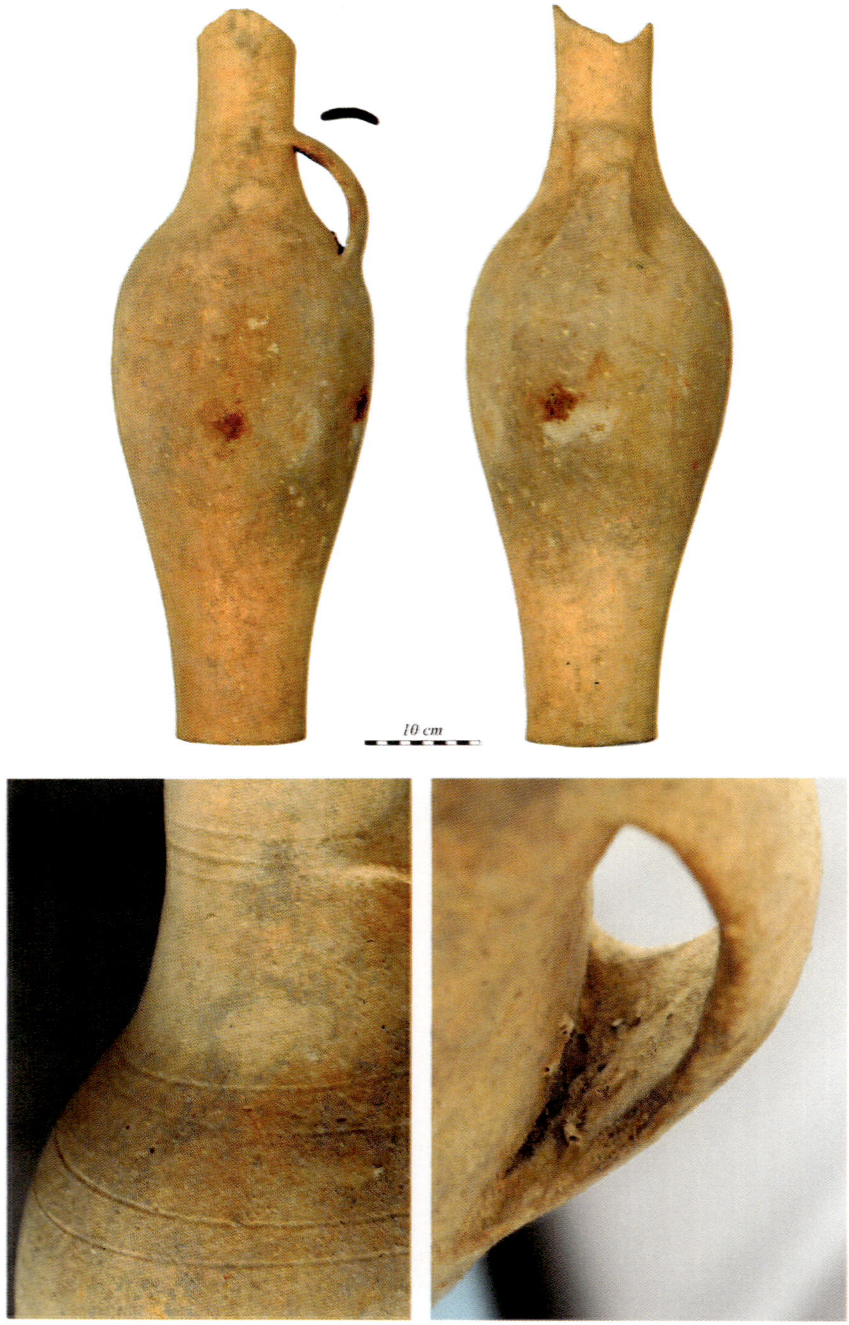

Plate 60. Tmutarakan jug from the museum's old collection, originally housed in the Pervane madrasah (Cat. no. 60)

Plate 61. Tmutarakan jug from the Sanctuary of Diogenes, US radar station, Sinop (Cat. no. 61)

Plate 62. Tmutarakan jug from the Black Sea, purchased from Nurettin Saral (Cat. no. 62)

Plate 63. Tmutarakan jug from the Black Sea, purchased from Tayfun Güner (Cat. no. 63)